Troubleshooting Windows Server with PowerShell

Derek Schauland
Donald Jacobs

Apress®

Troubleshooting Windows Server with PowerShell

Derek Schauland
Greenville, Wisconsin, USA

Donald Jacobs
Appleton, Wisconsin, USA

ISBN-13 (pbk): 978-1-4842-1850-1
DOI 10.1007/978-1-4842-1851-8

ISBN-13 (electronic): 978-1-4842-1851-8

Managing Director: Welmoed Spahr
Lead Editor: Gwenan Spearing
Development Editor: Douglas Pundick
Technical Reviewer: Adam Driscoll
Editorial Board: Steve Anglin, Pramila Balen, Louise Corrigan, Jim DeWolf, Jonathan Gennick, Robert Hutchinson, Celestin Suresh John, James Markham, Susan McDermott, Matthew Moodie, Douglas Pundick, Ben Renow-Clarke, Gwenan Spearing
Coordinating Editor: Melissa Maldonado
Copy Editor: Kim Burton-Weisman
Compositor: SPi Global
Indexer: SPi Global
Artist: SPi Global

Distributed to the book trade worldwide by Springer Science+Business Media New York, 233 Spring Street, 6th Floor, New York, NY 10013. Phone 1-800-SPRINGER, fax (201) 348-4505, e-mail orders-ny@springer-sbm.com, or visit www.springer.com. Apress Media, LLC is a California LLC and the sole member (owner) is Springer Science + Business Media Finance Inc (SSBM Finance Inc). SSBM Finance Inc is a Delaware corporation.

For information on translations, please e-mail rights@apress.com, or visit www.apress.com.

Apress and friends of ED books may be purchased in bulk for academic, corporate, or promotional use. eBook versions and licenses are also available for most titles. For more information, reference our Special Bulk Sales–eBook Licensing web page at www.apress.com/bulk-sales.

Any source code or other supplementary material referenced by the author in this text is available to readers at www.apress.com. For detailed information about how to locate your book's source code, go to www.apress.com/source-code/.

Printed on acid-free paper

For Laura—thanks for the encouragement.

For Nyla—keep learning.

Contents at a Glance

Contents

Contents

About the Authors

Derek Schauland is a Microsoft MVP with 18 years' experience configuring everything from Windows NT 4.0 environments to Windows Server 2016. He has worked in help desk and systems administrator roles helping companies and end users alike handle the challenges that can accompany the Windows experience. He has written for publications ranging from white papers for internal publication, to *Redmond Magazine* and *TechRepublic*, and books for Microsoft Press. When he isn't helping configure development or cloud environments, writing for the next great publication, or working to put on local technology events, he can be found tasting the latest craft beer, watching movies, or spending time with family and friends.

Donald Jacobs began his IT career back when Windows NT was the biggest and best new technology in the field. Since that time, he has earned a multitude of Microsoft certifications, including MCSE Server Infrastructure 2012, MCSA Office 365, MCITP Enterprise Administrator 2008, and MCTS for Windows 7. He has taught Microsoft's Certified PowerShell and Windows Server courses as a Microsoft Certified Trainer. Currently, Donald supports clients and customers with Microsoft products, particularly PowerShell, Azure, Office 365, Active Directory, Exchange, and Windows Server. In his downtime, he enjoys spending time with his family, watching hockey, and playing Dungeons & Dragons.

About the Technical Reviewer

Adam Driscoll is a senior software developer for Concurrency, Inc. and a PowerShell MVP based out of Madison, WI. He has experience working with a range of Microsoft technologies and programming languages. Adam is the author of the open-source project PowerShell Tools for Visual Studio. This extension is used by thousands of developers around the world and currently ships as part of the Visual Studio 2015 installation package. Adam is an avid blogger, a published author, a poor golfer, and a triathlete.

Acknowledgments

Derek Schauland: I would like to thank the academy—just kidding. In all seriousness, I would like to thank my friends, family, and colleagues, who have helped me learn enough to be dangerous and encouraged me to take on evermore challenging tasks. I would also like to thank Donn Jacobs for helping me to get this thing off the ground and doing the real work, Mike Halsey and the team at Apress for seeing this as awesome right off the bat, and the countless others who helped out along the way.

Donald Jacobs: With the support of many, this book came to be. To my parents, for helping me evolve into the person I am today. To Derek, for convincing me to do this project and for bringing me outside of my comfort zone. To my customers and clients, who helped me write PowerShell for everything and anything IT related. To Carrie, U+1F48B, and then some. And lastly, to Starbucks, for keeping me caffeinated through the writing process.

Introduction

Who this Book Is For

This book is intended for the system administrators and IT staff who are in charge of keeping the lights on. It may also assist grandma with an afternoon nap, but that is purely coincidental. We intend for readers to take this book and use it to help solve everyday problems in real environments. The fact remains that PowerShell is here to stay and should be something that is easily accessible, learnable, and shareable, and that is the overall goal of *Troubleshooting Windows Server with PowerShell*.

From college graduates in their first job to seasoned enterprise administrators, the content in this book is designed to help you learn how to use PowerShell. Maybe that is something as simple as get-command or update-help, and if so, that's ok. Each chapter is built to dig into different components of Windows Server and to help you develop skills to improve your Windows environment. Welcome to PowerShell. Let's go learn something new.

What You'll Learn

Each chapter is designed to take an aspect of Windows and delve into the components that you need to know. This book is about finding information quickly and determining what changed from the last time you documented your servers.

In Chapter 2, you learn how to read the event log and information that can be gleaned from each log. You'll learn how to create an HTML report to share what you discover in the event logs.

In Chapter 3, you'll start building documentation for computers, such as disk space, shares, NTFS permissions, and the hardware that is in use. We'll look at gathering information from Windows Management Instrumentation using both WMI and CIM queries.

Now that you understand the basics for your computers, in Chapter 4, we'll show you how to get a list of installed applications from your computers. Also in this chapter, we talk about comparing an old report to a new report to find which programs were added, deleted, or changed from the last report. This is very useful information for environments using change management.

In Chapter 5, we look at gathering information about Windows patches that were installed on your computers. You'll gather information using WMI and CIM. Along those lines, we look at learning if the computer is waiting for a reboot, or at the last reboot for your computers.

In Chapter 6, we look at current processes, starting and stopping processes, and emailing a report of processes to recipients. This information is great for determining what is running and starting processes required for management.

Like processes, in Chapter 7, we look at services on a computer, both local and remote. We start by listing the current status, then at starting and stopping services, and services that have dependencies. Again, reports to others are important, so we show you how to create a CSV file and share that information with email recipients.

In Chapter 8, we talk about how you can improve the examples shown in the book. We cover building PowerShell modules, Desired State Configuration, PowerShell remoting, and PowerShell scheduled jobs. This is the chapter in which you take what you learned in the book, and make it better and make it your own.

CHAPTER 1

Getting Started

It's early Friday morning, and you are still waking up from a cozy sleep when your phone rings. It's the company that you work for, informing you that a primary server is having problems and not functioning as expected. So, time to wake up and figure out what happened to the server.

Did it get rebooted? Was a patch installed last night? And, ultimately, what changed? That is always the big question: "What changed?"

With tools like Windows PowerShell—and the release of PowerShell Web Access—you can now start troubleshooting and, hopefully, start resolving Windows problems from outside your network.

This book is dedicated to essential first steps to help the IT administrator start troubleshooting Windows Server and figure out what changed. The first tool used should not be the built-in GUI tools; it should be PowerShell, especially as more things happen with Windows that don't involve the graphical user interface. PowerShell allows the IT administrator the ability to remotely troubleshoot a server and figure out what happened.

Note All of the source code used in this text is separated by chapter and made available online by visiting http://www.apress.com/971484218501.

This chapter kicks things off the book and gives you, the reader, a chance to see the authors' style and how we use PowerShell. Since PowerShell is a product that helps manage other products that make life easier for Windows system administrators, it does not have just one use. While working on this project, several alternate methods of doing things with Active Directory came suddenly to mind. Some of them sped up things that we were used to doing another way.

This book is meant to be a reference tool; this chapter is just a warm up for the things to come. Enjoy the ride.

Electronic supplementary material The online version of this chapter (doi:10.1007/978-1-4842-1851-8_1) contains supplementary material, which is available to authorized users.

Getting to Know PowerShell

Having a set of PowerShell commands at the ready will help when you get that phone call. So the first thing to look at is how long the computer has been running. So, you type the following command:

```
Get-WmiObject Win32_OperatingSystem -ComputerName Server1 | Select-Object @
{Name = 'LastStartTime' ; Expression = {[Management.ManagementDateTime
Converter]::ToDateTime($_.LastBootUpTime)}}
```

But realistically, that command isn't one that you can quickly remember and understand at 3:00 AM. You were ready for this, though, and you created a function that allows the same command with shorter syntax, something like this:

```
Function Get-TSUptime {
param ($ComputerName = $env:COMPUTERNAME)
$WmiOS = Get-WmiObject Win32_OperatingSystem -ComputerName $ComputerName
[Management.ManagementDateTimeConverter]::ToDateTime($WmiOS.LastBootUpTime)
}
```

It is much easier to type Get-TSUptime rather than the first example.

In this book, we will talk about how to get the basic information and how to convert some of the commands into functions. Once you have a lot of functions, you can build modules of common functions.

This book is designed to help you write your own PowerShell commands and use them to troubleshoot your environment. Because each environment is unique, this book helps you figure out what your organization needs.

What works for one company, may not necessarily work elsewhere. This book lets you know what to monitor and how to set up some of your troubleshooting tools.

Much of PowerShell is backward compatible to allow scripts written on a Windows 10 computer to operate in previous versions of Windows. We have tested the examples in this book with Windows 10, Server 2016, Server 2012 R2, and Windows 8.1. It is possible that many of these scripts will work in other versions of the operating system, but we have not tested them there. In addition, the examples provided here are "as is" with no warranty provided. Use them at your own risk—preferably in a lab to help you build tools that you can then use in production. We have done testing, but your mileage may vary depending on your environment. Some PowerShell cmdlets will only be available in later versions and we will make sure to mention which cmdlets work with what versions of operating systems.

This book is not the definitive answer to troubleshoot all Windows problems, but rather a guide to help you build your own tools.

GUI Tools vs. PowerShell

Microsoft has shipped GUI tools to administer Windows and other applications for as long as Windows has been around. Active Directory Users and Computers (ADUC) is a great example of one of these tools. How does it stack up against PowerShell? Let's find out.

Let's open ADUC and PowerShell to examine the differences. We need to make a couple of assumptions to get started. To follow along completely, you should run Active Directory Domain 2012 and your client computer should be Windows 8.

■ **Note** Windows Server 2012 and Windows 8 are no longer the current release. We will try to stay with the currently released version of both the server and client OS where possible. When we deviate from that, we will point it out, but in general, you should assume our examples are Windows 10 and Windows Server 2012 R2.

You should also have Remote Server Admin Tools installed because, let's face it, ADUC isn't part of the default tools on a client operating system. You can find the tools at `http://www.microsoft.com/en-us/download/details.aspx?id=39296`.

So, quickly modify a user's description … and … go!

Using ADUC: (1) Right-click your Active Directory domain. (2) Click Find. (3) Enter the user's login name. (4) Right-click the user name. (5) Click Properties. (6) Click in the Description field and enter a description. (7) Click OK. (8) Close the Find window.

■ **Note** By the way, using Active Directory Administrative Center (ADAC), introduced in Windows Server 2008, is faster than ADUC. Most people running a 2008 domain do not use this new and improved GUI. In some cases, the older tools work just as well; in other cases, people have simply not heard of the new tools. Search for "ADAC" or "Active Directory Administrative Center" to check it out.

See how easy that was? Now let's try the same thing in PowerShell.

Using PowerShell, type `Set-ADUser djacobs -Description 'Sales at BigCompany'` and hit Enter. Done!

So, which way is faster?

In many cases, PowerShell will be faster once you get the hang of it, but there is a bit of a learning curve to the new method. We will do our best to help you get moving with the command syntax for troubleshooting Windows. After reading this book, we hope that you will be inclined to first try things with PowerShell and only use the GUI to check your work.

For those of you who have touched PowerShell before and are curious why we didn't import any modules to run the previous code, PowerShell versions 3 and higher do not require the modules to be imported first; you can load them on the fly when cmdlets are used. For those of you who don't know what a cmdlet or a module are, keep reading.

Another example is when someone in your organization's HR department gives you an Excel file and they want you to update several fields for all users: telephone numbers, offices, descriptions, titles, and managers. Using ADUC, you can spend days updating those fields for all of your users, depending on the size of the environment. And, for those of you with many users, we hope that it doesn't take you days to complete.

Using PowerShell, data can be gathered directly from Excel or it can be saved as a CSV file within Excel into an array. You can loop through and modify the data for all users on the list within seconds.

OK, now the critics out there will be saying, yeah, but it took you 30 minutes to write the code, add error checking, and create an HTML report of any errors and successes to send back to HR in an email. Yes, it did, but next month when HR sends another Excel file with more users to be updated, just rerun the script and go get a cup of coffee, or tea, or your beverage of choice. The good news is that you can spend a minute deciding what to drink and still be done before you start those clickety-click changes using ADUC.

And for those of you thinking, "by the hour, not by the job," that is a true statement. However, those people are also still writing batch files to map drives for their users during login (don't get us started on that one). Those are the people who are telling their bosses how long it takes to do this stuff and expecting sympathy because they are so overworked.

Work smarter, not harder. Use PowerShell.

The Basics of PowerShell

There are many articles, classes, and videos on the basics of PowerShell. Hopefully, by now, you have taken advantage of these resources because this book assumes that you are familiar with the basics and want to expand your current knowledge.

PowerShell has cmdlets that are in "verb-noun" form. This book discusses some of the commands for finding information on computers—either workstations or servers. We build on the verb-noun cmdlets and use simple functions to give more power to the cmdlet.

■ **Note**   The nouns in PowerShell are singular nouns—get-process, for example. You can use plural nouns in functions, but you see a warning about unapproved verbs. They still work, but you will be warned.

Working with Variables

PowerShell comes with some built-in variables and allows others to be specified as needed like any other language. The biggest difference is that the variables do not need to be declared before they are used. Using a variable in PowerShell simply requires $myvariable = "hello reader" to be called. This populates $myvariable with the string value "hello reader".

The built-in variables (of which there are many) and any variables created during use are stored in a special drive called *variable*. Accessing this drive, which is only available to PowerShell, called a *PSDrive*, can be done by running "cd variable" from the command line. The context of the console changes. You can list all the variables currently stored in the PSDrive using a cmdlet such as Get-ChildItem, or aliases such as dir or ls.

CMD Is Dead—Long Live PowerShell

PowerShell is very much a replacement for cmd.exe and as such has commands and aliases for its commands that mirror those found in the command shell. In addition to aliases for cmd.exe commands, PowerShell also supports aliases for commands found in other shells. PowerShell can also run executables directly from the PowerShell console or Integrated Scripting Environment (ISE), just like the regular command line.

For example, the PowerShell way to list the contents of a folder is

```
Get-ChildItem -Path 'c:\users\username'
```

This displays all the folders and files stored inside the profile directory for the specified user. Running Get-ChildItem without a path lists the items in the current folder. In the Windows command shell, running dir lists the contents of the current folder. dir was created as an alias for Get-ChildItem, which makes it a shortcut, or alias, for the full function.

Another alias for Get-ChildItem is ls, which is also used on the *nix operating systems. PowerShell incorporates these things to maintain both backward compatibility and platform commonality, allowing users of other platforms to work with PowerShell. Aliases can be created for functions or cmdlets written by PowerShell users or third parties. Like variables, aliases are stored in a PSDrive and can be listed as needed. Simply use cd alias: to access the alias drive within PowerShell.

Why All the Drives?

We have seen two PowerShell drives (also known as PSDrives) so far in this section: alias and variable. These built-in drives help PowerShell behave like a file system style explorer. This way, these things can be accessed just like the C: drive and have contents listed, written, modified, or deleted as such. There are a number of PSDrives in PowerShell; some just might surprise you, like the PSDrives registry. A detailed discussion of these items is beyond the scope of this book, but a brief introduction might prove very useful for troubleshooting.

Listing the PSDrives is as easy as executing Get-PSDrive. Figure 1-1 displays the output of the command.

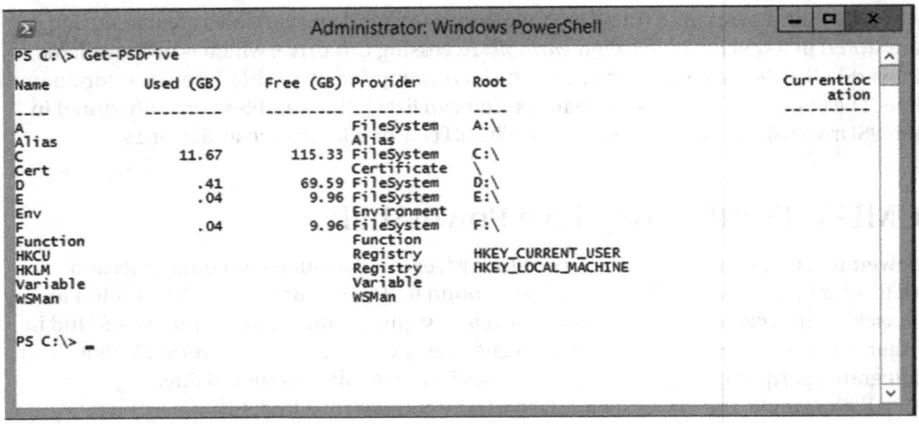

Figure 1-1. *Get-PSDrive*

■ **Note** Other items may be added to PSDrives just like variables, aliases, and other objects. Providers that can be added are of type registry, alias, Environment, File System, Function, and Variable.

The Natural Progression of Tool Building

Tool building starts with something simple: a problem that needs to be fixed and resolved. Once you identify a problem, you need to find PowerShell cmdlets to solve that problem. Use the built-in PowerShell help feature to find cmdlets that will help you solve problems. Once you find these cmdlets, test them to determine the best way for them to fix the problem.

Bigger problems take several cmdlets used together to solve problems. They can be saved in a script or function to repeatedly solve a problem. Adding parameters to your scripts or functions allow these scripts to be used in other environments.

As more scripts and functions are created, adding them into modules keeps them organized. Typically, a module is a set of related Windows PowerShell tools that can be loaded into memory for the current PowerShell session.

Typically, each module contains common scripts that help solve your bigger goals; in our example, we could have a module for troubleshooting Windows with PowerShell. Earlier, we used a single PowerShell command to find the last start time of a computer. Then, we decided we wanted to be able to run that against other computers, so we built a function called Get-TSUptime. For a quick check, let's create another simple function called Get-TSFreeSpace (this example is explained later in the book).

```
Function Get-TSFreeSpace {
  [CmdletBinding()]
  param ($ComputerName = $env:COMPUTERNAME)
  $allDisks = Get-WmiObject -ComputerName $ComputerName -Class Win32_
  LogicalDisk -Filter "DriveType='3'"
  foreach ($disk in $allDisks) {
    $results += [PSCustomObject]@{
      'ComputerName' = $disk.DeviceID
      'FreeSpace(GB)'= $([int]($disk.FreeSpace / 1GB))
      'Size(GB)'= $([int]($disk.size / 1GB))
    }
  }
  $results
}
```

Now that we have two common functions, we can save them into a module. In this book, we are creating and testing modules inside the Documents folder of the current user. The way that you create a module is to simply create a folder called TSTools at C:\Users\<YourUserID>\Documents\WindowsPowerShell\Modules and then save both functions inside another script called TSTools.PSM1 inside the TSTools folder that you just created.

Once you are done with that, if you are starting PowerShell v4 or later, the TSTools module automatically loads inside your PowerShell current session. If you want to load this module manually, you can simply call the command Import-Module TSTools and it then loads all of the functions within the TSTools.PSM1 module into the current session.

■ **Tip** You can view the current module path within a PowerShell environment by running $env:psmodulepath. This environment variable displays the current paths where modules can be stored. When stored here, the modules can be loaded by using import-module ModuleName. Adding folders to the module path is also possible and it is discussed later in this book.

As you create and complete more functions, you can add them to existing modules that share a common purpose.

PowerShell Is Not Going Away

Microsoft has made large commitments with PowerShell, which will keep it in the forefront for quite some time. Previous scripting and command shell environments were focused on accomplishing tasks and automating things, but they lacked security in many areas. PowerShell takes security seriously, so seriously, in fact, that scripts will not run by default.

Microsoft has also added several extra security features, including module logging, script block logging, and transcription. These features are available in PowerShell version 5 and they can be configured in PowerShell version 4, with some other upgrades.

Microsoft has also done a lot of security using constrained endpoints for PowerShell sessions. Constrained endpoints allow you to declare which cmdlets are available for specific users and groups. As an example, you can set up a PowerShell endpoint configuration that only allows cmdlets that start with Get to be executed for users of the help desk group.

Another new feature for securing PowerShell is a relatively new concept called Just Enough Administration (JEA), which provides role-based access control (RBAC). Microsoft has actually used features of JEA when managing Exchange for a while, but JEA is a great way to start implementing fine-grained controls on your computers.

What Does this Do for PowerShell?

The ability to manage the growing majority of applications and services that run an environment from PowerShell make working at scale much faster and easier. The built-in scalability of this technology is amazing. The third-party adoption of the technology is also a statement that PowerShell is a great technology. Although third-party solutions are outside the scope of this book, many environments may benefit from some of them. Here are a few resources that you can check out to see what types of third-party products are out there:

- vSphere PowerCLI: http://www.vmware.com/support/developer/PowerCLI/index.html

- Amazon AWS Tools for Windows PowerShell: https://aws.amazon.com/powershell/

- PowerShell for Veeam Backup & Replication: http://www.veeam.com/blog/powershell-for-veeam-backup-replication.html

As you can see, adoption of PowerShell is not just for administrators anymore; third-party companies and other tools can leverage PowerShell to improve manageability.

Chapters in this Book

Throughout this book, we talk about several key areas of Windows computers. In the early chapters, we discuss Windows event logs, gathering information about your servers, and finding installed applications on your servers.

While looking at the event logs, we'll talk about listing all the event logs and searching for a specific event id or keyword. We'll also talk about how to export data from event logs into reports for viewing as a web page and emailing the reports to others.

As we gather information about servers, we'll examine the disks on the servers and the free space on those disks. We'll also get a list of file shares on the server. We'll examine NTFS permissions on folders and files, getting current values on setting new NTFS permissions. We'll show you how to find hardware information about your devices, both locally and remotely. As a bonus section, we'll talk about the difference between using WMI and CIM to query remote servers.

We'll cover how to find information, and compare a report of installed applications from today with a report saved a while ago to find out which applications have been added, removed, or changed.

Along with applications, we'll talk about Windows updates, gather information about hotfixes on your computer, and discuss whether you should use WMI or CIM to get the information. You'll also learn how to uninstall a hotfix should you ever find the need to do so. We'll also talk about pending restarts of your computer.

Toward the end of the book, we'll look at processes and services. We also talk about creating modules, Desired State Configuration, PowerShell remoting, and PowerShell scheduled jobs.

Processes are programs running on your computer. We'll look at finding information about processes, again, on the local computer and remote devices. We'll also show you how to start and stop processes. After that, we'll look at how PowerShell interacts with services, including stopping, starting, and the aspects of working with them.

Assumptions Used in this Book

Benny Hill said it best about when people assume things. So, we are going to try to clarify several aspects of this book that may be confusing to some. It's best if we can simply clarify some of our idiosyncrasies right away, instead of readers trying to guess what we meant.

All the functions have a TS prefix on the cmdlet noun.

Many times, we see too many people creating a function called "Get-FreeSpace", which is not wrong. It follows the verb-noun standard that Microsoft has created for function names. This works great and nothing is wrong with calling your function Get-FreeSpace, except that it is a very small way to look at solutions.

Scenario: Two users create a function called Get-FreeSpace and you have them both on your computer. How do you know whose function you are using? They are similar but not the same, and the name does not tell whose function it belongs to. One way to distinguish which function is what is to add a prefix to the noun. We have seen things like initials of the author (Get-DJFreeSpace), or a company abbreviation if used within a company (Get-TSTools). Now, if you share your function with the world, you have just distinguished your function from others.

All PowerShell cmdlets that we use will be run "as Administrator".

In the real world, running an elevated session of PowerShell (or one "as Administrator") in normal day-to-day operations is not recommended, but for simplicity and to ensure that you get the same results as shown in the book, please elevate your PowerShell session by making sure that you run "as Administrator". To do this, right-click the PowerShell icon and select Run as Administrator.

Once you have tested your script and you know that things are working as expected, try running your script without elevated permissions to see if things still work. You will find that most items work fine without elevated permissions, but for testing, we are going to be running elevated commands.

Write-Host is not a puppy killer.

Sometimes, we want to display a simple message on the screen. We don't need to do anything more yet since we are just testing or just displaying output to the screen. In day-to-day scripts, we do not use `Write-Host` unless testing, and we remove them during the final revision of the script.

It is nice to create a simple test like this:

```
if ($test -eq $true) {
    Write-Host "Good test" -ForegroundColor Green
} else {
    Write-Host "Failed test" -ForegroundColor Red
}
```

With this example, you can simply read the output or check the color of the text on the screen. It is very easy to see a success (green) or a failure (red) simply by glancing and seeing the output. Again, most of our day-to-day scripts do not use `Write-Host`, but for testing, definitely use it, and if the script is only to display data to the screen, please use this to help in testing.

PowerShell version 5 has added a new cmdlet called `Write-Information`, which improves `Write-Host`. Along with `Write-Information`, PowerShell has added `-InformationVariable` to `Write-Host`, which allows you to save information from the `Write-Host` to a variable to recall later, or to save your output, instead of just sending the information to the PowerShell session that called it (see Figure 1-2).

```
Administrator: Windows PowerShell                                                    —  □  ×
PS C:\Reports> Write-Host "Found a Process called '$(Get-Process pow* | Select-Object -ExpandProperty Name)'"
  -InformationVariable ProcsThatStartWithPow
Found a Process called 'powershell'
PS C:\Reports>
PS C:\Reports> $ProcsThatStartWithPow
Found a Process called 'powershell'
PS C:\Reports>
PS C:\Reports> _
```

Figure 1-2. *Adding Write-Information to Write-Host*

■ **Tip**   To write output to the screen in a production script, consider using `write-verbose`, which displays the items to the screen if the verbose switch is supplied. If the `-verbose` switch is not specified, no screen output displays.

How to Let PowerShell Help You Learn More

PowerShell supports comment-based help that can be extremely useful in teaching users more about how to work with PowerShell. This is good for the built-in cmdlets that ship with the environment, because you can ask PowerShell for more information about how things work and how to use certain cmdlets. As an example, `Get-Help Get-Command` explains how the `Get-Command` cmdlet works, including the parameters required and available, as well as examples for usage of the cmdlet. Figure 1-3 shows the help for `Get-Command`.

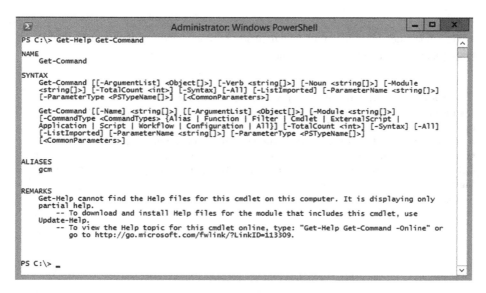

Figure 1-3. *Help for the Get-Command cmdlet*

■ **Note**   Your output may be a little different based on your operating system and if you have updated your help files. Figure 1-3 has not updated the help files yet.

With PowerShell, Microsoft has made a point of improving usability and learnability. In other Windows applications, the F1 button generally brings up something similar to a manual containing a bunch of documentation. Get-Help does this for PowerShell, but it goes further because the help is comment based. This allows anyone writing PowerShell scripts, functions, or modules (all of which are covered in the coming pages) to include help for their PowerShell code.

For many help items, when PowerShell is first installed—on a new Windows 10 machine, for example—the help does not contain much, if any information. Microsoft does not include the full help contents in current releases of the operating systems, but allows you to use the Update-Help cmdlet to ensure that your cmdlets are always current.

Update-Help must be run in an elevated shell, but goes out to the Internet and collects the help for cmdlets and functions with the ability to accept updateable help. Using a help system in this way allows updates to happen at any time, rather than just when an update to PowerShell ships.

If something needs to change, the author can modify the online help file to add an example or change the wording of the content. The next time that Update-Help is run, the new information is collected.

■ **Tip** It is a good idea to update help regularly, because things do change from time to time. This can be done by simply running update-help in an elevated shell.

In an environment in which computers cannot (or should not) reach the Internet, the updateable help content can be downloaded and saved to a location within the environment by using a cmdlet called Save-Help. Here the Update-Help cmdlet can be pointed at the offline help location, allowing these computers to get help updates. Once you have updated your local help files, you can run a command such as Get-Help Get-Command, which displays the help contents for the Get-Command cmdlet, as seen in Figure 1-4.

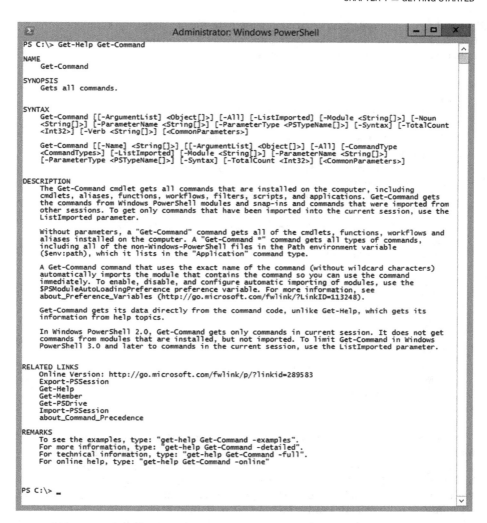

Figure 1-4. *Help for Get-Command after updating help commands*

Using a specially defined set of comments at the top of a script, file or function, the Get-Help cmdlet can read the comments and display them on the screen. The following is an example of the structure of comments for help:

```
<#
    .SYNOPSIS
        Description of the function.
    .DESCRIPTION
        A detailed description of the function.
    .PARAMETER  ParameterA
        The description of the ParameterA parameter.
    .PARAMETER  ParameterB
        The description of the ParameterB parameter.
    .EXAMPLE
        Get-Something -ParameterA 'One value' -ParameterB 32
    .EXAMPLE
        Get-Something 'One value' 32
    .INPUTS
        System.String,System.Int32
    .OUTPUTS
        System.String
    .NOTES
        Additional information about the function go here.
    .LINK
        about_functions_advanced
    .LINK
        about_comment_based_help
#>
```

This comment structure works by filling in the sections for each item. The heading for each area describes what is contained below it. The headers—including the period at the beginning and the blank line between sections—are required for the comment-based help to work. The help is built to make adding instructions easy so that more PowerShell users will make use of the feature to learn more about the language (scripting environment or application) and to improve the readability of their code. Remember, automation and reusability are a focus of PowerShell; the comment-based help is one way to ensure its adoption within an environment.

The following completes the comment block to build help into your PowerShell code:

```
<#
    .SYNOPSIS
        This function updates titles in Active Directory
    .DESCRIPTION
        Using this function will update the title of a user in Active Directory
    .PARAMETER  UserName
        The username parameter identifies the record in Active Directory to
        be updated
```

```
.PARAMETER  Title
    The title parameter corresponds to the title attribute in Active Directory.
.EXAMPLE
    Update-TSADUserTitle -UserName 'user' -Title "PowerShell Wizard"
.EXAMPLE
    Update-TSADUserTitle 'user' "PowerShell User"
.INPUTS
    System.String
.OUTPUTS
    System.String
.NOTES
    Use this function to update the title of an Active Directory user
.LINK
    about_functions_advanced
.LINK
    about_comment_based_help
#>
```

This shows the completed help for PowerShell code; it updates the title for a specified user within Active Directory. Some of the portions of help block have not been modified; they are not necessarily required, but can be completed if your PowerShell code requires it.

As you work through the examples and build PowerShell scripts, be sure to consider using help. It ensures that the script is extremely usable and allows others to pick up the code and dive right in, extending the usability even further.

PowerShell also provides help in line with the code that it assists. Although this works, it does not make for readable code. Consider placing help at the top of the script or function.

Remember, PowerShell has an enormous amount of data and information available to anyone willing to look for it. Using Get-Help in the PowerShell console gets information about any cmdlet or properly formed function that the console is aware of. Along with that, the about_Functions web page (https://technet.microsoft.com/en-us/library/hh847829.aspx) is the online version of a PowerShell help file; you can view about_Functions in the console by passing them to Get-Help. Get-Help about_Functions returns information in the console, whereas the web page shows similar information at TechNet. In some cases, using the –online switch opens help in a browser, as long as the URI is filled in within comment-based help.

Summary

In the introductory chapter, we introduced Microsoft PowerShell and discussed how the authors of this book use it. We looked at some of things that we consider important in the use of PowerShell in day-to-day work. A few of these things fly in the face of the way others might use or the guidance they provide. Having many different ways to accomplish tasks with PowerShell is part of its strength and we hope you are ready to get into PowerShell.

In Chapter 2, we dive into events management using Windows PowerShell. Throughout the book, examples will build upon previous chapters, where possible; this way, a complete picture and module of what has been covered is created for those who choose to follow along.

More Reading

PowerShell about_Functions: https://technet.microsoft.com/en-us/library/hh847829.aspx

Approved Verbs for Windows PowerShell Commands: https://technet.microsoft.com/en-us/library/ms714428.aspx

Windows PowerShell Scripting: https://technet.microsoft.com/en-us/scriptcenter/dd742419.aspx

CHAPTER 2

■ ■ ■

Managing the Windows Event Log

Windows is a complex application, to say the least. Things happen that the user is aware of—for example, starting Microsoft Word—and things happen that the user may not be aware of, such as a privilege audit of a security access to a file on the C drive. In the latter case, the person sitting at the computer sees the folder open or an error about access being denied. The event log contains a record of these events to keep administrators informed about what actions are being taken on a computer.

In many cases, the logs will not be used to review the starting or stopping of Microsoft Word because this is fairly benign, but sometimes the timestamp captured to the log might be useful in figuring out why Word does not start. In this chapter, we examine how to get ahold of the events generated by Windows and other applications using PowerShell.

What Can Windows Capture?

Microsoft Windows captures more information about what is going on within a system than is likely to fit (nicely) within the pages of this book. Not only does it record things that are in error, but also things that might be a problem (warnings) and even service stops and starts (informational messages). There is a plethora of information captured to the event log.

As the Windows operating system evolves and new iterations are released, the items captured and the number of logs used to store this information continues to grow. In one of the later builds of Windows 10 (10240), there are five standard Windows logs, but there are countless more under the Applications and Services Logs folder. Most of these pertain to Windows internal applications and services and they are not used in general troubleshooting for the operating system, but it's nice to know they exist.

In addition to these logs and the entries they contain, you can create logs and log entries for specific things you need to keep track of. We will look into that at the end of this chapter.

© Derek Schauland, Donald Jacobs 2016
D. Schauland and D. Jacobs, *Troubleshooting Windows Server with PowerShell*,
DOI 10.1007/978-1-4842-1851-8_2

Accessing the Event Log Information

We know that PowerShell is the scope of this book—and there will be a fair amount of it coming up, first though, you should know where to look to find an event using the Event Viewer (eventvwr.msc) built-in tool. The reason for this is to show you what an event contains so that you can tailor PowerShell to access it and return just what you are expecting. This saves the hassle of combing through piles of output in the console to chase down the things that you need.

■ **Note** PowerShell is a great tool, but it can be even greater when used to manipulate data that you already understand. Starting in the Event Viewer helps with that.

Figure 2-1 lists the details of an event, showing the time when the computer was shutdown. As you can see, there is the text description about the shutdown, but there is also the event id, log name, event source, and other useful information.

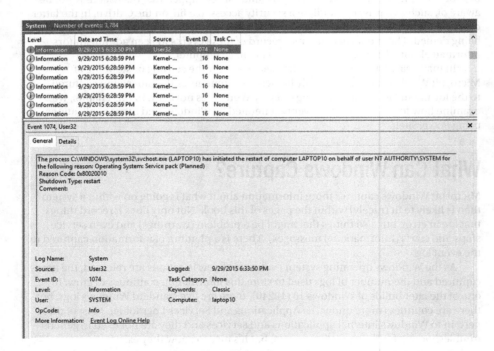

Figure 2-1. *A system shutdown event in the Event Viewer*

Finding this information in the event log with PowerShell might look something like this:

```
Get-EventLog -LogName System | Where-Object {$_.Eventid -eq 1074}
```

You will notice that there are several events appearing and that they are all the same event—a shutdown. But which is the event found in Figure 2-1? From the bit of PowerShell used here, there is nothing that tells which is the precise event.

To get to the specific event shown, we need to give PowerShell a bit more information; but getting there is certainly possible.

Get-EventLog

When working in PowerShell, it is often times useful to start with broad results and work your way toward the specific, unless you know exactly what you are after right up front. For example, you might chase down information about an Active Directory computer object by specific name because you know you want to work with Engineering-PC, but in the case of an event log, working your way toward the specific result might be more useful. In addition to getting more familiar with PowerShell and the event log, you might come across additional information that serves your purpose and you can make a note to collect for later use.

We find PowerShell to be the land of opportunity when it comes to learning the tools and syntax; getting in there and doing it or using the shell is very helpful.

Now that you have seen the event log in the Event Viewer and in PowerShell, we can consider the information that we are going to collect using PowerShell. To do this, a scenario might work best because we have useful information to collect and for which to produce a report.

Scenario

As a systems administrator, Geoff gets a fair amount of questions about applications and servers within his environment. His boss generally asks him about the performance statistics of the E-mail server every day. Geoff is used to the questions from his boss, but he still finds himself chasing down the data.

He is looking for a way to produce a summary list of information regarding the E-mail server and wants to see information about this server from the event log. He has been reading a lot about PowerShell online and wonders if it will get him the information that his boss regularly requests.

That is the goal of this chapter: to find an easier method of getting the information requested of Geoff. The data can be reviewed as is, but it should also be placed in a report that can be quickly reviewed when Geoff's boss inquires. Creating a report file allows you to email the information to anyone who might find it useful, such as Geoff's boss and fellow team members.

Finding Information with PowerShell

Two cmdlets come to mind when considering ways to get things out of the Windows event log:

- Get-EventLog

- Get-WinEvent

The Get-EventLog cmdlet provides a list of information from the specified log that meets the specified criteria. As shown in Figure 2-2, the output is a list of the events requested by the following command:

Get-EventLog -LogName System -Newest 10

```
Windows PowerShell                                                    —    □    ×
PS C:\reports> get-eventlog -logname system -Newest 10

Index Time          EntryType   Source            InstanceID Message
----- ----          ---------   ------            ---------- -------
 5397 Oct 31 09:21  Information Microsoft-Windows...        19 Installation Successful: Windows successfully i...
 5396 Oct 31 09:21  Information Microsoft-Windows...        43 Installation Started: Windows has started insta...
 5395 Oct 31 09:21  Information Microsoft-Windows...        98 The description for Event ID '98' in Source 'Mi...
 5394 Oct 31 09:21  Information Microsoft-Windows...        43 Installation Started: Windows has started insta...
 5393 Oct 31 09:21  Information Service Control M... 1073748864 The start type of the Windows Modules Installer...
 5392 Oct 31 09:21  Information Microsoft-Windows...         1 The system has returned from a low power state....
 5391 Oct 31 09:21  Information Microsoft-Windows...        23 NIC /DEVICE/{1FB9A83F-FF34-45C5-A80F-1130SD569D...
 5390 Oct 31 09:21  Information Microsoft-Windows...        21 Media connected on NIC /DEVICE/{1FB9A83F-FF34-4...
 5389 Oct 31 09:21  Information Microsoft-Windows...        24 NIC /DEVICE/{1FB9A83F-FF34-45C5-A80F-1130SD569D...
 5388 Oct 31 09:21  Information Microsoft-Windows...        24 NIC /DEVICE/{1FB9A83F-FF34-45C5-A80F-1130SD569D...

PS C:\reports>
```

Figure 2-2. *Capturing the newest 10 system logs*

We chose -newest 10 here to keep the returned output as short as possible. If you leave it out and run Get-EventLog -LogName System, you should see quite a bit of data scroll past.

Get-EventLog | Get-Member returns the properties for Get-EventLog as output:

- Category

- CategoryNumber

- Container

- Data

- Entrytype

- Index

- InstanceID

- MachineName

- Message

- ReplacementStrings

- Site

- Source

- TimeGenerated

- Timewritten

- UserName

- EventID

When the command is executed with no formatting parameters, PowerShell displays the output as a table if there are fewer than five parameter values returned for an item. If there are five or more values returned, the default output is a list. In this case, there are 11 items, so a table of results is shown.

The items shown are what were deemed most useful by the creators of the cmdlet, but you can pull out any information available, either in addition to or instead of what is listed by default.

By default, when running Get-EventLog -LogName System -Newest 10, we got a table showing Index, Time, EventType, Source, InstanceID, and Message. These are pretty good to start with, but what if the event occurred but it was not written immediately, or if you wanted to know the categoryNumber instead of the InstanceID?

To do that, you pipe the results of your original cmdlet to the Select-Object cmdlet and change the values returned.

```
Get-EventLog -LogName System -Newest 10 | Select-Object -Property Index,
TimeGenerated, TimeWritten, EventType, Source, CategoryNumber, Message
```

This builds a table showing the properties you asked for in the select portion of the statement shown in Figure 2-3.

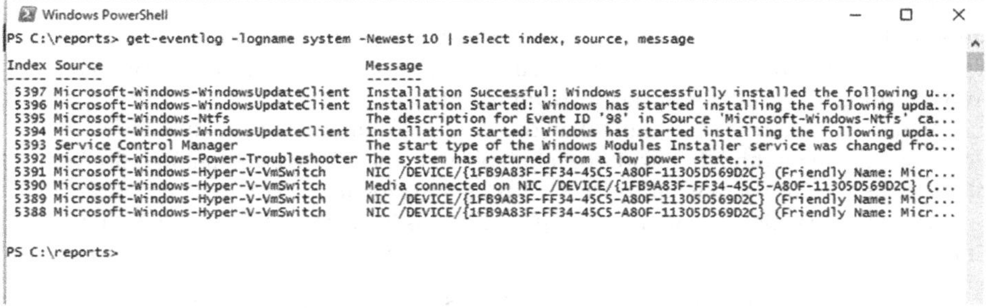

Figure 2-3. *Selecting different properties for event log entries*

Get-WinEvent

Get-WinEvent is similar to Get-EventLog, but supports different properties (or names the properties differently with the same information). In addition, Get-WinEvent does seem to perform significantly faster when hitting remote systems.

■ **Note**   The -FilterHashTable parameter filters the cmdlet results by value pairs in a hash table. Supplying the names and their associated values speeds up the filtering process. In addition to the filtering being improved, some of the typing needed is reduced (or at least moved). This parameter only works on Windows 7 and Server 2008R2 and later versions of Windows operating systems. You have to use the -FilterXml parameter on older Windows versions.

In addition, Get-WinEvent manages the XML formatting of the event logs of Windows Vista and newer releases of Windows. Get-EventLog is great for simple and quick local queries, but Get-WinEvent seems much more responsive when used on remote computers.

The simple act of telling PowerShell that you would like specific properties returned is just one of the ways that PowerShell can help you find and analyze information.

Being able to get to the event log and pull back information helps you with creating reports that can show at a glance what is going on in the machines' event logs.

Why Choose One cmdlet over Another?

Sometimes the choice of which cmdlet to use depends on what properties you are going to retrieve. Other times, the parameters accepted by the cmdlet might influence your choice; for example, many cmdlets in PowerShell support the -ComputerName parameter, which allows them to be executed against remote computers. Some cmdlets do not support this parameter and so other methods need to be employed to use them on other systems. Performance might be another reason to choose one cmdlet over another. Another thing to consider is backward compatibility.

Remember, there is often more than one way to accomplish a particular task in PowerShell. The method that works best for you and is easiest to understand is the best place to start. Building on what you learn is part of the fun of working with PowerShell.

You can see which parameters a cmdlet supports by reviewing the cmdlet's help. Entering Get-Help Get-EventLog returns one of two things:

- The stub help for the cmdlet, which is very sparse and may appear to be missing information. This means that your help needs to be updated. Running Update-Help cmdlet in an elevated shell downloads the latest help from Microsoft.

- The basic help for the cmdlet; it contains an overview of what the cmdlet can do and the syntax that might be used. Adding the -Detailed, -Full, or -Example parameters to the Get-Help line shows more information about the cmdlet.

Getting Logs from Remote Computers

As mentioned earlier, sometimes you need to gather log information from remote computers. Since it is unlikely that you are using a server to do your job (and you shouldn't be), you want to connect to one or more servers to retrieve information and produce some kind of output that others in the organization can understand. If people have trouble gleaning anything from the report, they will not use it and will continue to ask for assistance. Until now, the focus has been generally about the event log and how a systems administrator accesses a log for information, which is great if all the managed systems are local and there is no need to work with computers in far-flung locations. This section gets you started on access to event information on remote computers.

To execute a cmdlet against a remote computer, you do not need to remote desktop into the system or physically connect to it; typically, you can use the -ComputerName parameter of the cmdlet you want to run. This passes the cmdlet to the specified computer and retrieves the information from that system, rather than your local computer. For example, if we needed to get the system log information from a system named Server01, the following PowerShell command gets us what we need:

```
Get-EventLog -ComputerName Server01 -LogName System
```

When executed, that command connects to Server01 and retrieves the system event log, similarly to the previous command run against the local system.

You could also use Get-WinEvent -ComputerName Server01 -LogName System to access the remote computer's log information. Comparing the performance of each using Measure-Command shows quite a performance improvement by Get-WinEvent on remote computers, but your mileage may vary with regard to performance testing.

The following uses Get-WinEvent and Get-EventLog while measuring performance:

```
Measure-Command {Get-WinEvent -LogName Application}:
1 second 510 milliseconds
Measure-Command {Get-EventLog -LogName Application}:
0 seconds 310 milliseconds
```

Both of these results were taken from the local event log. On a remote machine, the results were as follows:

```
Measure-Command {Get-WinEvent -ComputerName remote -LogName Application}:
22 seconds 118 milliseconds
Measure-Command {Get-EventLog -ComputerName remote -LogName Application}:
44 seconds 718 milliseconds
```

Now that the information has been collected, let's do something useful with the data.

Shaping the Gathered Information

Raw event log data pulled back to PowerShell is not terribly useful, since it just scrolls past as fast as it is returned. With modifications, like selecting certain events or a set number of items, this may change somewhat because only the information specifically asked for is returned. Looking at five records in the PowerShell console is not so bad, but five thousand might be more work than its worth.

Now that we know how to get the information out of the event log, we can sculpt the results to display them in a friendlier format. PowerShell has cmdlets for formatting that can help with this, aside from just Format-List or Format-Table.

Returning to our previous example, we can build a formatted file that Geoff can use to review information found in the event logs of various machines within his organization. Because there was no formatting guideline specified, the data can (and should) be as flexible as possible. Providing output options for the data allows the individuals using it to work with it in a variety of ways.

Comma-Separated Values

Many applications can pull information from comma-separated values (CSV) files to improve processing and allow further data analysis to happen. If a database application needs to have information quickly imported for new products, a CSV file can list all of these products and then get imported to avoid lengthy inserts or updates to the system.

PowerShell is good at CSV. It can both generate and accept input from a CSV file, making this a great place to start.

In the case of event log reporting, a CSV can provide an input file for a database or other applications that can work with event log data. It is also fairly simple to create.

You start out by gathering the information that you need from the event log:

```
$systemlog = Get-EventLog –LogName System –Oldest 10
```

Notice that the values were put into the systemlog variable. This was done only to park the data for the time being; it is not required for a CSV file to be created.

With the data in a variable, it can be piped to the select-object cmdlet to choose the properties desired; from there, it can be turned into a CSV by piping the results to another cmdlet: Export-csv.

To step through the process, take the contents of the systemlog variable and pipe it to Select-Object.

```
$systemlog | Select-Object -Property InstanceId, Message, Source, TimeGenerated
```

Figure 2-4 shows the output of this command.

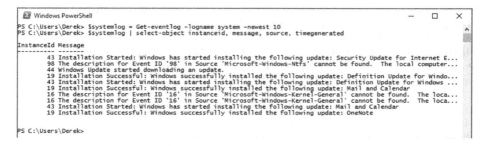

Figure 2-4. *Specifically selected properties from the event log*

From here, the CSV can be generated using this selection, as you can see in Figure 2-5.

```
$systemlog | Select-Object -Property InstanceId, Message, Source,
TimeGenerated | Export-Csv -Path "c:\reports\systemlog.csv"
```

⁄	A	B	C	D	E	F	G	H	I	J	K
1	#TYPE Selected.System.Diagnostics.EventLogEntry										
2	InstanceId	Message	Source	TimeGenerated							
3	19	Installatio	Microsoft	10/10/2015 9:03							
4	43	Installatio	Microsoft	10/10/2015 9:03							
5	16	The descri	Microsoft	10/10/2015 9:03							
6	16	The descri	Microsoft	10/10/2015 9:03							
7	19	Installatio	Microsoft	10/10/2015 9:02							
8	43	Installatio	Microsoft	10/10/2015 9:02							
9	16	The descri	Microsoft	10/10/2015 9:02							
10	16	The descri	Microsoft	10/10/2015 9:02							
11	19	Installatio	Microsoft	10/10/2015 9:02							
12	43	Installatio	Microsoft	10/10/2015 9:02							
13	16	The descri	Microsoft	10/10/2015 9:02							
14	16	The descri	Microsoft	10/10/2015 9:02							
15	44	Windows	Microsoft	10/10/2015 9:02							
16	44	Windows	Microsoft	10/10/2015 9:02							
17	19	Installatio	Microsoft	10/10/2015 9:02							
18											

Figure 2-5. *A CSV file created from event log data*

You may notice something odd at the top of the CSV file: a message about TYPE shown in the first line of the file. This is object information about the CSV; it really doesn't affect the data in the CSV at all. It is not something that has to be placed to help others determine the type of data that was exported. If you import the CSV file back into PowerShell, that tells PowerShell how to interpret that data. To remove that line of extra information, you can use the -NoTypeInformation switch on the Export-Csv cmdlet:

```
$systemlog | Select-Object -Property InstanceId, Message, Source,
TimeGenerated | Export-Csv -Path "c:\reports\systemlog.csv"
-NoTypeInformation
```

This suppresses that line from being added. If you re-execute the command with the new switch added, you may see an error in the PowerShell console. If the file is open, it cannot be rewritten by Export-Csv; closing the existing file and executing the command solves the problem.

The new, cleaner CSV file is shown in Figure 2-6.

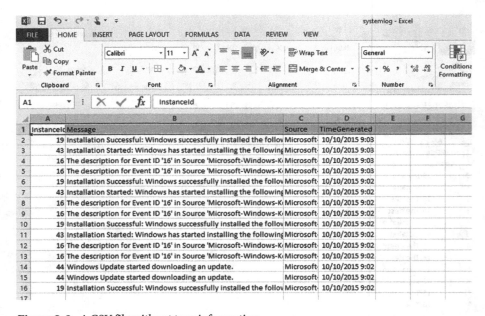

Figure 2-6. *A CSV file without type information*

Now we have generated a CSV file with the newest 10 entries in the system log. It can be opened in Notepad or in Microsoft Excel for viewing, or it can be imported into something else for processing.

Creating an HTML Report

Comma Separated Values files are nice and certainly have their usefulness, but when providing a report to management, they aren't very appealing. With HTML output and formatting for things like SQL Reporting Services gaining popularity, people are well used to seeing data in a web-based format. They generally also find navigating this type of information simple and straightforward.

PowerShell can do this too, almost as easily as creating a CSV file.

■ **Note**   Creating HTML output is as simple as creating CSV files; however, with a bit of tweaking, the style and presentation of HTML data generated by PowerShell can be quite improved.

Remember, the `systemlog` variable still has the raw objects returned from the system log in the event log. This simplifies the process, or at least takes the redundancy out. This variable is stored in memory until the current PowerShell console closes. Once you close the current PowerShell console, all the variables used in that session are removed from memory. In addition, a variable can be overwritten with a new value, or simply removed by using `Remove-Variable <variablename>` to clear the contents.

■ **Note**   You can store variables, functions, and other frequently used things in your PowerShell profile, but configuring profiles is beyond the scope of this book.

What Else Can Be Done with this Information?

Once the output formatting is done (in our case as a CSV file or an HTML file), the next step is to either use the data in another application or script in PowerShell (in the case of the CSV) or dress up the data and push it out to HTML to be shared with others. This section goes through other types of formatting for information gathered from the event log, keeping in mind that much of the information gathered will need to be shared with colleagues.

Formatting HTML for Readability

Sending objects to an HTML file puts a basic formatting together that is very usable, but adding some formatting to alternate the row colors or put a more appropriate header and title on the document can bring some level of professional appearance to the document.

To put some formatting together for the file, we can define the header data as a Here-String variable. Then fill it full of all kinds of HTML header information, as shown here:

```
$htmlformat = @"
<style>
Table {border-width: 1px; border-style: solid; border-color: black;}
TH {border-width: 1px; padding: 3px; border-style: solid;}
TR:nth-child(even) {background: #CCC}
TR:nth-child(odd) {background: #FFF}
</style>
"@
```

■ **Note** The Here-String in PowerShell is a way to include multiple lines of text "as is" within a single variable, without the need for line breaks, carriage returns, or other weird formatting. Using Here Strings allows you to pass this block of text as a variable to other code—plain and simple. Just include @" "@ as a wrapper around the text to include.

This way, the HTML file can be formatted using the stylesheet elements specified by PowerShell; the resulting output just includeS the styles.

Next up, since the event log data is already contained in a variable called systemlog, we can work on passing this data around a bit and converting it to HTML.

```
$HTMLformatted = $systemlog | ConvertTo-Html –fragment | Out-String
```

This set of code passes the event log information captured to the ConvertTo-Html cmdlet and produces a fragment of HTML, which is then converted to a formatted string and passed to a function (coming next) that prepares the formatting and other things to be displayed. Essentially, it applies CSS styling to the table and alternates the row color for display.

HTML Formatting with a Function

The function below can be used (and reused) to process the information collected across systems and output the data in a very useful HTML format for use at a later time or inclusion in an email.

```
Function Get-TSHtmlReport
{
        [CmdletBinding()]
        param (
                [Parameter(Mandatory = $true)]
                [ValidateSet("System", "Application", "Security")]
                [string]$LogName,
                [Parameter(Mandatory = $true)]
                [string]$SaveFile
        )
```

```
        Begin
        {
                $htmlformat = @"
<style>
Table {border-width: 1px; border-style: solid; border-color: black;}
TH {border-width: 1px; padding: 3px; border-style: solid;}
TR:nth-child(even) {background: #CCC}
TR:nth-child(odd) {background: #FFF}
</style>
"@
                $HTMLhead += "<H1>Event log information from
                $($env:COMPUTERNAME)</H1>"
                $HTMLhead += "<H2>Log name: $($LogName)</H2>"
        }
        Process
        {
                $events = Get-EventLog -LogName $LogName -Newest 50 |
                Select-Object -Property Index, EventID, Message
        }
        End
        {
                $events | ConvertTo-Html -head $HTMLhead -body $htmlformat |
                Out-File -FilePath $SaveFile
        }
}

}
```

The information passed to the formatting function is manipulated as a string, HTML, or XML data that is presented in a well-formatted HTML table.

We are not quite done yet; the body of the document, the titles, and other things still need some preparation. Remember, the preceding function just handles the table rows.

With the formatting completed, the data is ready to be pushed out to an actual file. Simply passing the entire bit of information out to the file will do nicely.

Please note that this is a bit more than is minimally needed to get things out to an HTML file; you can simply run the data out to a file:

```
$systemlog | Select-Object Eventid, Message | Convertto-Html | Out-File "c:\
reports\unformatted-system-log.html"
```

Both of these open in a browser and display the contents of the system log; however, the function includes formatting to draw the attention of the reader to the table.

Figures 2-7 and 2-8 show the unformatted and formatted HTML files, respectively.

| ← | → | ↻ | file:///C:/powershell/systemlog.html | | ⊡ |

InstanceId	Message
19	Installation Successful: Windows successfully installed the following update: Microsoft Solitaire Collection
43	Installation Started: Windows has started installing the following update: Microsoft Solitaire Collection
16	The description for Event ID '16' in Source 'Microsoft-Windows-Kernel-General' cannot be found. The local computer may not have the necessary registry information or you may not have permission to access them. The following information is part of the event:'199', '\?? \C:\Users\Derek\AppData\Local\Packages\Microsoft.MicrosoftSolitaireCollection_8wekyb3d8bbwe\Microsoft.MicrosoftSolitaireCollection_3.4.9241.0_x64__8w '0', '0'
16	The description for Event ID '16' in Source 'Microsoft-Windows-Kernel-General' cannot be found. The local computer may not have the necessary registry information or you may not have permission to access them. The following information is part of the event:'199', '\?? \C:\Users\Derek\AppData\Local\Packages\Microsoft.MicrosoftSolitaireCollection_8wekyb3d8bbwe\Microsoft.MicrosoftSolitaireCollection_3.3.9211.0_x64__8w '47', '6'
19	Installation Successful: Windows successfully installed the following update: MSN Sports
43	Installation Started: Windows has started installing the following update: MSN Sports
16	The description for Event ID '16' in Source 'Microsoft-Windows-Kernel-General' cannot be found. The local computer may not have the necessary registry information or you may not have permission to access them. The following information is part of the event:'162', '\?? \C:\Users\Derek\AppData\Local\Packages\Microsoft.BingSports_8wekyb3d8bbwe\Microsoft.BingSports_4.6.169.0_x86__8wekyb3d8bbwe\ActivationStore\Activ
16	The description for Event ID '16' in Source 'Microsoft-Windows-Kernel-General' cannot be found. The local computer may not have the necessary registry information or you may not have permission to access them. The following information is part of the event:'162', '\?? \C:\Users\Derek\AppData\Local\Packages\Microsoft.BingSports_8wekyb3d8bbwe\Microsoft.BingSports_4.5.168.0_x86__8wekyb3d8bbwe\ActivationStore\Activ
19	Installation Successful: Windows successfully installed the following update: MSN Money

Figure 2-7. *An unformatted HTML file*

Index	EventID	Message
4737	44	Windows Update started downloading an update.
4736	19	Installation Successful: Windows successfully installed the following update: Definition Update for Windows Defender - KB2267602 (Definition 1.207.3759.0)
4735	43	Installation Started: Windows has started installing the following update: Definition Update for Windows Defender - KB2267602 (Definition 1.207.3759.0)
4734	19	Installation Successful: Windows successfully installed the following update: Mail and Calendar
4733	16	The description for Event ID '16' in Source 'Microsoft-Windows-Kernel-General' cannot be found. The local computer may not have the necessary registry information or message DLL may not have permission to access them. The following information is part of the event:'198', '\?? \C:\Users\Derek\AppData\Local\Packages\microsoft.windowscommunicationsapps_8wekyb3d8bbwe\microsoft.windowscommunicationsapps_17.6310.42251.0_x64__8wekyb3d8bbw '0', '0'
4732	16	The description for Event ID '16' in Source 'Microsoft-Windows-Kernel-General' cannot be found. The local computer may not have the necessary registry information or message DLL may not have permission to access them. The following information is part of the event:'198', '\?? \C:\Users\Derek\AppData\Local\Packages\microsoft.windowscommunicationsapps_8wekyb3d8bbwe\microsoft.windowscommunicationsapps_17.6306.42251.0_x64__8wekyb3d8bbw '604', '76'

Figure 2-8. *A formatted HTML file*

■ **Note**   A quick note about formatting and other general PowerShell tricks. This book focuses on troubleshooting with PowerShell, and although some other functions that help with formatting are shown, these are not the focus of the book. The authors may use these in examples and code samples to help call attention to certain information. These things may also help when using these reports to present information to others.

With the HTML file (formatted or unformatted) created, we can do all kinds of interesting things with it. If Geoff's boss wants to see the report first thing every morning, that can be arranged as well. By using another cmdlet and an internal email server (or even a Gmail account, if needed), a report can be attached to an email and delivered to the boss every morning.

■ **Note**   You could use scheduled tasks to automate some of the things that we are doing here. We touch on scheduling tasks later in this book.

Recall that we were going to get the newest 10 items from the system log on the specified computer and return it for analysis. Once returned to a variable in PowerShell, we formatted it as a CSV and a formatted HTML file. Then we emailed the file to the boss at 5:15 every morning (working overnight may or may not make Geoff appear industrious).

If we put the whole thing together in a script, it might look like the following sample:

```
        Function Get-TSHtmlReport
{

        [CmdletBinding()]
        param (
                [Parameter(Mandatory = $true)]
                [ValidateSet("System", "Application", "Security")]
                [string]$LogName,
                [Parameter(Mandatory = $true)]
                [string]$SaveFile
        )
        Begin
        {
                $htmlformat = @"
<style>
Table {border-width: 1px; border-style: solid; border-color: black;}
TH {border-width: 1px; padding: 3px; border-style: solid;}
TR:nth-child(even) {background: #CCC}
TR:nth-child(odd) {background: #FFF}
</style>
"@
                $HTMLhead += "<H1>Event log information from
                $($env:COMPUTERNAME)</H1>"
                $HTMLhead += "<H2>Log name: $($LogName)</H2>"
        }
        Process
        {
                $events = Get-EventLog -LogName $LogName -Newest 50 |
                Select-Object -Property Index, EventID, Message
        }
        End
        {
                $events | ConvertTo-Html -head $HTMLhead -body $htmlformat |
                Out-File -FilePath $SaveFile
        }
}
Get-TSHtmlReport -LogName System -SaveFile C:\Reports\test2.html

Send-mailmessage –to geoff@company.com, boss@company.com –from reports
@company.com –smtpserver smtp.company.com –subject "Events Report" -body
"Attached is the most recent events report" -attachment "c:\reports\test2.html"
```

31

The function outputs a file on the desktop following that the Send-MailMessage cmdlet sends the generated file to Geoff and his boss. This is fairly straightforward and extremely useful.

Can PowerShell Use the Event Log to Store Information?

So far, this chapter has mainly covered getting information for analysis out of the event log on Windows systems, but we should also look at putting data into the event log. PowerShell can certainly do that, and in some cases, this might be the best place to park information related to an application or process until you need it for later analysis.

To put information into an event log, you can use the following cmdlet:

```
Write-EventLog -LogName Application -Source "My Application" -EventID 1000
-Message "This is the message being logged"
```

As you will notice, there is an error when running this cmdlet. This happens because "My Application" is not a valid source that exists in the Application event log. This is fairly easy to fix: simply adding it as a valid source in the chosen log solves the problem.

```
New-EventLog -LogName Application -Source "My Application"
```

Adding the "My Application" source to the Application log allows events to be added to the log.

Putting data into the event log carries as much difficulty as getting it out. Sure, you need to pay attention to tags, sources, and log names, but that is true on the way out as well. It helps to ensure that you can find the data later when it is needed again.

Another advantage to logging information to the event log is that other administrators may use that as a starting point for their troubleshooting. If information from your PowerShell adventures is tracked there as well (with details and contact information), then the issues that may arise with scripts will be easy to locate and correct.

Even though PowerShell is capable of writing to the event log, like everything else, there is a place for doing so. If we write log information about a Windows process or application, we put it in the log; many times, this is a separate sublog of the application or item that we're dealing with. If logging the action(s) of a PowerShell script, however, a simple folder of text files works. This does a few things:

- Keeps the PowerShell script logs out of the way

- Allows them to be cleaned up more frequently than flushing an event log

- Keeps things simple

Could you put it in the event log? Sure, but if scripting against a dozen computers, there should be a central location for the logs that is easily remembered and shared with other staff members. It also ensures a central location for things related to scripting.

> ■ **Note**   Centralized event log storage is possible and it can be configured fairly quickly.
> See http://blogs.technet.com/b/wincat/archive/2008/08/11/quick-and-dirty-
> large-scale-eventing-for-windows.aspx for more information on this topic.

Keeping script logs out of the event logs feels cleaner, especially since script logs are only occasionally used for troubleshooting, and scripts are generally not always logged.

If your organization has a good grasp on centrally managed event logs (or they require such tracking), by all means, use the event log for script data storage.

With the use of Get-WinEvent, Get-EventLog, and Write-EventLog, the administrator has a decent arsenal of tools to help troubleshoot Windows Server or workstation issues that may come up. PowerShell's strengths include its remoting capabilities and its willingness to manipulate information for use by other PowerShell scripts, functions, or modules, and by other applications or employees within the organization.

Summary

In this chapter, our focus was the event log. We looked at some of the ways that PowerShell helps access information in the logs. In addition, we touched on certain constructs like filter hash tables, which provide another way of using PowerShell's features.

In the next chapter, we will look at gathering and reporting system information from a Windows system.

CHAPTER 3

Gathering and Reporting Detailed Information from a Computer

Another day, another chapter. Wait, strike that. Another day, another server. Sometimes it is nice to know how a server is doing today so that later, when the same server is having problems, you can compare data to historical data.

Consider this scenario: You get a phone call saying that Server01 is having problems. You jump on the server and document the basics of the computer, disk space, shares, NTFS permissions, and computer settings. Great! But now the question is: What changed?

Without anything to compare to, you have no idea what changed since the last time that you documented. Clearly, it's important to have good documentation of what a server is doing today, so that when a problem arises in the future, you have something to compare your results to.

Gathering Disk Space

There are a few ways to gather disk space, such as using Windows Management Instrumentation (WMI) and native cmdlets on later versions of PowerShell. The native cmdlets, Get-Disk and Get-PhysicalDisk, return information about the whole disk, but do not return information about logical disks.

In this next part, we will check disks visible to the operating system and we will only return basic information about the disks.

© Derek Schauland, Donald Jacobs 2016
D. Schauland and D. Jacobs, *Troubleshooting Windows Server with PowerShell*,
DOI 10.1007/978-1-4842-1851-8_3

Disks First

Let's look at the disk commands Get-Disk and Get-PhysicalDisk, shown in Figure 3-1.

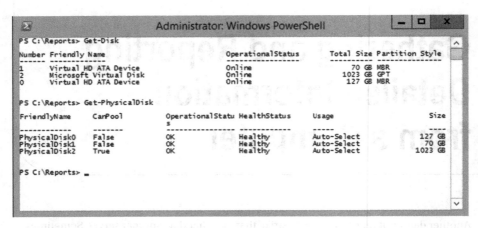

Figure 3-1. *Get-Disk and Get-Physical Disk*

Both commands show simple output and the disks that the server can currently see and access. This data should be stagnant. Export this to CSV or HTML and record this data. Save it and use it when needed. We can add this data into a module to gather other information about the server, but for the moment, let's save it to CSV and HTML just to record the data.

```
Get-PhysicalDisk |
    ConvertTo-Html -Title 'Get-PhysicalDisk Information' |
    Set-Content C:\Reports\GetPhysicalDisk.htm

Get-PhysicalDisk |
    Export-Csv -NoTypeInformation -Path C:\Reports\GetPhysicalDisk.csv

Get-Disk |
    ConvertTo-Html -Title 'Get-Disk Information' |
    Set-Content C:\Reports\GetDisk.htm

Get-Disk |
    Export-Csv -NoTypeInformation -Path C:\Reports\GetDisk.csv
```

This saves the data to both CSV and HTML files.

Logical Disks

PowerShell does not yet have a cmdlet to capture logical disk information, so we will use WMI calls to find the logical disk information. Windows Management Instrumentation is a core Windows management technology that can be used to manage both local and remote computers. WMI provides a consistent approach to carrying out day-to-day management tasks. (We're using WMI rather than CIM (Common Information Model in this example, but the difference is explained later in this chapter.)

The commands we need to know about are Get-WmiObject and Get-CimInstance. Once we have looked at those commands, we need to examine a WMI object.

The WMI objects that we will use are located within the Root\CIMV2 namespace. There are many classes under this namespace. To list all the classes, use the following command:

```
Get-WmiObject -List -Namespace ROOT\CIMV2 | Sort-Object Name
```

To find classes related to disk, filter down your choices by using the WHERE command, filtering for any WMI name that matches *disk*, like this:

```
Get-WmiObject -List -Namespace ROOT\CIMV2 | Where-Object Name -Match 'disk'
| Sort-Object Name.
```

There are a few classes that contain the name disk, and we're sure that you have tested a few of the returned values to figure out which class we want to work with, but we'll give you the answer to hurry this up: Win32_LogicalDisk.

Running the following command lists all types of disks that the computer knows about, as shown in Figure 3-2:

```
Get-WmiObject -Class Win32_LogicalDisk
```

Microsoft has limited built-in PowerShell documentation around the WMI classes, so the best place to find information about WMI is by using the MSDN website. The MSDN page for Win32_LogicalDisk is at https://msdn.microsoft.com/en-us/library/aa394173.aspx.

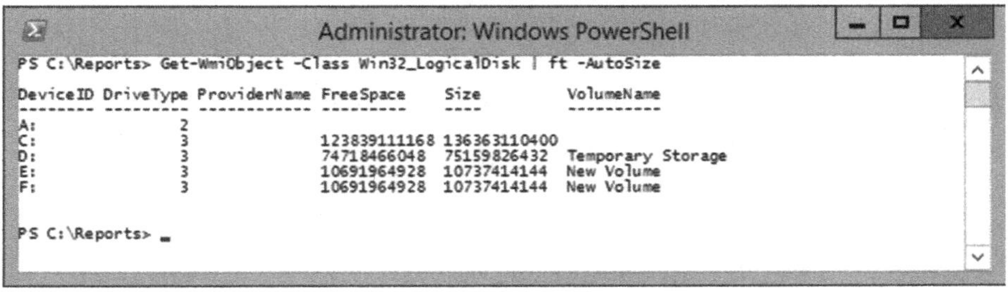

Figure 3-2. Get-WMIObject -Class Win32_LogicalDisk

But wow, who really wants to convert bytes to gigabytes in their head? Well, with PowerShell, you don't have to. As seen in Figure 3-3, PowerShell can convert bytes to gigabytes with minimal work.

```
Get-WmiObject -Class Win32_LogicalDisk |
    Format-Table DeviceID,
        DriveType,
        @{Name = 'FreeSpace(GB)' ; Expression = {$_.FreeSpace / 1GB}; FormatString = "N2"},
        @{Name = 'Size(GB)' ; Expression = {$_.Size / 1GB}; FormatString = "N2"}
```

Figure 3-3. *Get-WMIObject -Class Win32_LogicalDisk with advanced formatting*

We'll get a nice little table with related information. But again, who can remember this command each time? If you create a function around it, as shown in Figure 3-4, it'll be even easier to remember when you need it.

```
Function Get-TSDiskSizes {
    param ($ComputerName = "$env:COMPUTERNAME")
    Get-WmiObject -Class Win32_LogicalDisk |
        Format-Table DeviceID,
            DriveType,
            @{Name = 'FreeSpace(GB)' ; Expression = {$_.FreeSpace / 1GB}; FormatString = "N2"},
            @{Name = 'Size(GB)' ; Expression = {$_.Size / 1GB}; FormatString = "N2"},
            VolumeName
}
```

Figure 3-4. *Function Get-TSDiskSizes*

Now, checking our server that is having problems, we can quickly determine if the server is out of disk space.

Listing Shares

We don't have a good reason why shares disappear, but too often, it's human error. Most of the support calls around missing shares all start the same way: "I don't know what happened, but today, the share that all my users connect to is missing." Usually, it's caused by human error when an admin accidently deletes a share. So, let's just document the shares and save the data to a file.

Again, we need to use our new friends, WMI and CIM, to find the information. To find classes related to shares, filter down your choices by using the Where-Object cmdlet, filtering for any WMI name that matches *share*:

```
Get-WmiObject -List -Namespace ROOT\CIMV2 | Where-Object Name -Match 'share'
| Sort-Object Name
```

However, after looking at all the answers, you are going to want to use Win32_Share to get all of your information.

Let's look at the documentation on Win32_Share at MSDN (https://msdn.microsoft.com/en-us/library/aa394435.aspx). The important thing to notice is the TYPE of share. From the documentation, you can see the different types of shares returned, as shown in Table 3-1.

Table 3-1. *WMI Share Drive Types*

Disk Drive	0
Print Queue	1
Device	2
IPC	3
Disk Drive Admin	2147483648
Print Queue Admin	2147483649
Device Admin	2147483650
IPC Admin	2147483651

So, by listing all drives of the Disk Drive type, you can run this command:

```
Get-WmiObject -Class win32_share | Select-Object Name, Path, Description, Type
```

Save that information as part of a report, and if needed, you can come back later to verify that things are the same. Part of the reason we document servers is because you never know what information you will need later.

But wait, there's more! For people running newer versions of Windows operating systems, Microsoft has created some new cmdlets to simplify the management of servers. These new cmdlets are part of a module called SMBSHARE. As seen in Figure 3-5, running a cmdlet like Get-Command -Module SmbShare lists all the cmdlets within the module.

```
PS C:\Reports> Get-Command -Module SmbShare |
   Sort-Object -Property Name |
   Select-Object -Property Name, Source


Name                                         Source
----                                         ------
Block-SmbShareAccess                         SmbShare
Close-SmbOpenFile                            SmbShare
Close-SmbSession                             SmbShare
Disable-SmbDelegation                        SmbShare
Enable-SmbDelegation                         SmbShare
Get-SmbBandwidthLimit                        SmbShare
Get-SmbClientConfiguration                   SmbShare
Get-SmbClientNetworkInterface                SmbShare
Get-SmbConnection                            SmbShare
Get-SmbDelegation                            SmbShare
Get-SmbMapping                               SmbShare
Get-SmbMultichannelConnection                SmbShare
Get-SmbMultichannelConstraint                SmbShare
Get-SmbOpenFile                              SmbShare
Get-SmbServerConfiguration                   SmbShare
Get-SmbServerNetworkInterface                SmbShare
Get-SmbSession                               SmbShare
Get-SmbShare                                 SmbShare
Get-SmbShareAccess                           SmbShare
Grant-SmbShareAccess                         SmbShare
New-SmbMapping                               SmbShare
New-SmbMultichannelConstraint                SmbShare
New-SmbShare                                 SmbShare
Remove-SmbBandwidthLimit                     SmbShare
Remove-SmbMapping                            SmbShare
Remove-SmbMultichannelConstraint             SmbShare
Remove-SmbShare                              SmbShare
Revoke-SmbShareAccess                        SmbShare
Set-SmbBandwidthLimit                        SmbShare
Set-SmbClientConfiguration                   SmbShare
Set-SmbPathAcl                               SmbShare
Set-SmbServerConfiguration                   SmbShare
Set-SmbShare                                 SmbShare
Unblock-SmbShareAccess                       SmbShare
Update-SmbMultichannelConnection             SmbShare
```

Figure 3-5. *Get-Command -Module SmbShare*

So, for those of you running newer versions of Windows Servers, we'll explain how we would start getting information about servers. The preferred method is to use the newest cmdlets; but not all servers understand what these cmdlets are, so learning the new and the old ways of gathering information is critical in mastering troubleshooting Windows with PowerShell. A quick way to work with SMB share access is also included in this module. The noun for these access cmdlets is (drum roll) SmbShareAccess.

Figure 3-6 shows an example of listing local SMB share access permissions on the print$ share; it is simple enough to run and view the permissions.

```
PS C:\Reports> Get-SmbShareAccess -Name print$ | Format-Table -AutoSize

Name     ScopeName AccountName                    AccessControlType AccessRight
----     --------- -----------                    ----------------- -----------
print$ *           Everyone                       Allow             Read
print$ *           BUILTIN\Administrators         Allow             Full
print$ *           BUILTIN\Print Operators        Allow             Full
print$ *           BUILTIN\Server Operators       Allow             Full
```

Figure 3-6. *Get-SmbShareAccess output*

Trying to get share permissions on older servers is not easy, but it can be done using WMI and security descriptors. An example of this involves the Win32_LogicalShareAccess WMI class (https://msdn.microsoft.com/en-us/library/aa394186.aspx). So, running a quick query, as shown in Figure 3-7, against the local computer like this:

```
Get-WmiObject -Class Win32_LogicalShareAccess | Select-Object
SecuritySetting, Trustee, AccessMask
```

It returns results that are very similar.

```
PS C:\Reports> Get-wmiobject -class win32_LogicalshareAccess |
  where SecuritySetting -match 'print' |
  Select-Object -Property SecuritySetting, Trustee, AccessMask |
  Format-Table -AutoSize

SecuritySetting                                                      Trustee                                            AccessMask
---------------                                                      -------                                            ----------
\\IGDOMCON1\root\cimv2:win32_LogicalshareSecuritySetting.Name="print$" \\IGDOMCON1\root\cimv2:win32_SID.SID="S-1-1-0"    1179817
\\IGDOMCON1\root\cimv2:win32_LogicalshareSecuritySetting.Name="print$" \\IGDOMCON1\root\cimv2:win32_SID.SID="S-1-5-32-544" 2032127
\\IGDOMCON1\root\cimv2:win32_LogicalshareSecuritySetting.Name="print$" \\IGDOMCON1\root\cimv2:win32_SID.SID="S-1-5-32-550" 2032127
\\IGDOMCON1\root\cimv2:win32_LogicalshareSecuritySetting.Name="print$" \\IGDOMCON1\root\cimv2:win32_SID.SID="S-1-5-32-549" 2032127
```

Figure 3-7. *Win32_LogicalShareAccess output*

OK, that is not as clean as the output from Get-SmbShareAccess. You have to massage the data to convert the SID to a friendly name. You need to convert the AccessMask to a friendly name of the rights using a BITWISE operation, which we are not going to cover in this book. So basically, this is a good reason to make sure all of your operating systems are updated to the most current version; then you can just use the current cmdlets.

NTFS Permissions

The good news is that there are good cmdlets that let us examine and modify the Access Control Lists for files or folders: the Get-Acl and the Set-Acl cmdlets.

Getting the ACLs

Getting the actual data for a file or folder is pretty straightforward; by now, you can probably guess the pattern: `Get-Acl -Path C:\Reports`, as seen in Figure 3-8. Well, it's not so simple because we need to "autosize" the table and then wrap the columns to fit the data nicely to the screen.

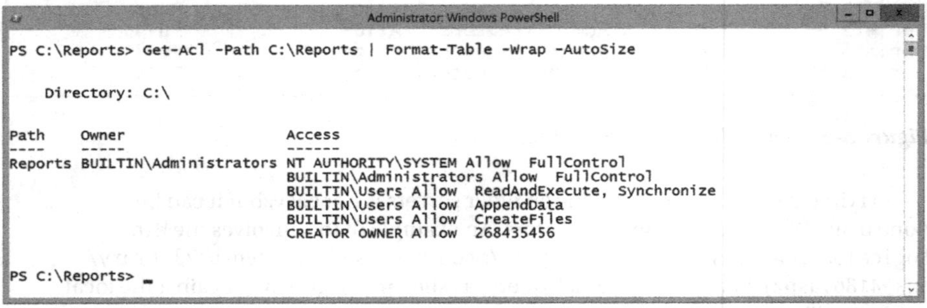

Figure 3-8. *Get-Acl*

But then to really look at the data, we need to parse out the `Access` property, and then this is as simple as grabbing the `Access` data and putting it into a table. The output of returning the `Access` property is shown in Figure 3-9.

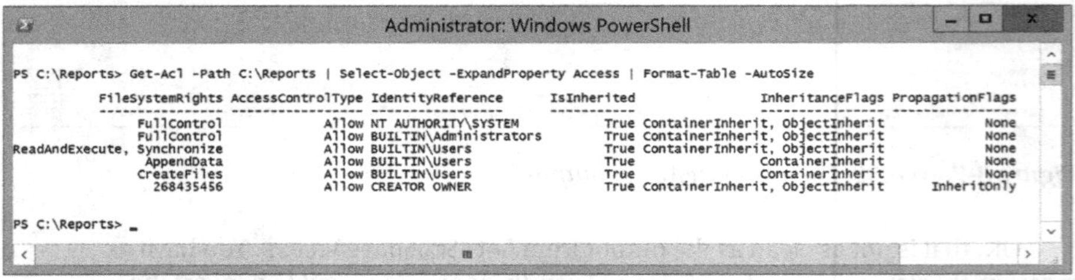

Figure 3-9. *Get-Acl Access expanded*

Another way to do that is to run the following command:

```
Get-Acl -Path C:\Reports |
    Select-Object -ExpandProperty Access |
    Format-Table -AutoSize
```

We can save that data in different formats, but it is nice to have this data on file and ready to see what changed.

Now that you have learned the built-in method for listing the permissions of a file or folder, here is a secret: you can do an Internet search for something like, "Microsoft script center PowerShell file system security" and maximize your time by using the tools that someone else has already put together.

Setting the ACLs

This is where you want to start strapping on the thinking cap, because setting an ACL on a file is not as easy as reading it.

Let's start by discussing the FileSystemAccessRule class, which "Represents an abstraction of an access control entry (ACE) that defines an access rule for a file or directory." (https://msdn.microsoft.com/en-us/library/system.security. accesscontrol.filesystemaccessrule.aspx).

Within the FileSystemAccessRule, we find the constructor that consists of IdentityReference, FileSystemRights, InheritanceFlags, PropagationFlags, and AccessControlType. A constructor is an access control rule that defines the user account rights that determine which actions are allowed or disallowed on computers running Microsoft Windows.

Hang on, this will make sense in a moment. We'll show you the commands that we use to create an ACE and apply it to a file using PowerShell. Then once you see the example, each section is explained to tell you what each line is doing.

```
$IdentityReference = New-Object System.Security.Principal.
NTAccount("MyDomain\Bob")
$FileSystemRights = [System.Security.AccessControl.FileSystemRights]::Read
$InheritanceFlags = [System.Security.AccessControl.InheritanceFlags]::None
$PropagationFlags = [System.Security.AccessControl.PropagationFlags]::None
$AccessControlType =[System.Security.AccessControl.AccessControlType]::Allow

$ACE = New-Object System.Security.AccessControl.FileSystemAccessRule (
    $IdentityReference,
    $FileSystemRights,
    $InheritanceFlags,
    $PropagationFlags,
    $AccessControlType
)

$CurrentACL = Get-ACL "C:\Reports\Test.ps1"
$CurrentACL.AddAccessRule($ACE)

Set-ACL -Path "C:\Scripts\Test.ps1" -AclObject $CurrentACL
```

■ **Note**   The order in which you create the first five variables is not important, but we're showing you the order as referenced by the FileSystemAccessRule constructor.

43

We start by creating the IdentityReference. In the example, we use the NetBIOS domain name and a SamAccountName for a user or group. This can also use SID, which is helpful when working in domain environments where the file server may be in a different Active Directory (AD) site than the Domain Controller (DC) that created user or group. In order for this to assign permissions, the SamAccountName needs to be converted to a SID by the file server. However, if you pass the SID to the file server, the ACL can be updated with the SID.

Then, we work on the FileSystemRights. This can be a comma-separated value such as "read, write". Information on enumerating the FileSystemRights is found at `https://msdn.microsoft.com/en-us/library/system.security.accesscontrol.filesystemrights.aspx`). The list is shown here.

- AppendData
- ChangePermissions
- CreateDirectories
- CreateFiles
- Delete
- DeleteSubdirectoriesAndFiles
- ExecuteFile
- FullControl
- ListDirectory
- Modify
- Read
- ReadAndExecute
- ReadAttributes
- ReadData
- ReadExtendedAttributes
- ReadPermissions
- Synchronize
- TakeOwnership
- Traverse
- Write
- WriteAttributes
- WriteData
- WriteExtendedAttributes

The InheritanceFlags determines the semantics of inheritance for access control entries (`https://msdn.microsoft.com/en-us/library/system.security.accesscontrol.inheritanceflags.aspx`). The following are possible values for it:

- ContainerInherit: The ACE is inherited by child containers, such as subfolders

- ObjectInherit: The ACE is inherited by child objects, such as files

- None

The PropagationFlags specifies how Access Control Entries are propagated to child objects. (`https://msdn.microsoft.com/en-us/library/system.security.accesscontrol.propagationflags.aspx`) The possible values for this are:

- InheritOnly: Specifies that the ACE is propagated only to child objects. This includes both container and leaf child objects.

- None: Specifies that no inheritance flags are set.

- NoPropagateInherit: Specifies that the ACE is not propagated to child objects.

The last option is to set the AccessControlType, which specifies whether an AccessRule object is used to allow or deny access (https://msdn.microsoft.com/en-us/library/w4ds5h86.aspx). There are only two options for this:

- Allow: The AccessRule object is used to allow access to a secured object.

- Deny: The AccessRule object is used to deny access to a secured object.

See how easy that is? Too easy. We still haven't created the ACE from the FileSystemAccessRule but building things one piece at a time helps keep things straight. Putting it all together to build the rule comes next.

Once you do that, we need to get the current security descriptor for the file or folder and that is done with the Get-Acl cmdlet. Then we add the new ACE rule we created to the security descriptor and finally, just reapply the ACL to the file using the Set-Acl cmdlet.

Now, this was not that bad, but only when working with a single file and each time you want to modify an attribute or value, you need to modify the script and then run the whole thing again. What you can do to make this usable against more than one file or folder is to build a function around the script.

And what kinds of things can you use as a parameter within your function? How about the Identity, rights, inheritance, propagation, control type, and file name? Yep, you guessed correctly. You can even get fancier within your function by using ValidateSet for some of your parameters.

■ **Note**   You can learn more about parameters within functions by using the help file Get-Help about_functions_advanced_parameters

---

[Déjà vu moment] Now that you have learned the built-in way to set permissions of a file or folder, understand that many might do an Internet search for something like, "Microsoft script center PowerShell file system security" and maximize their time by using the tools that someone else has already put together. The PowerShell community is a great source for information.

Hardware

This section is pretty straightforward (with a twist). So all of the hardware information can be pulled using WMI or CIM information. The version of the operating system that you are querying and the communication method to other computers determine if you use WMI or CIM. For the examples in this next session, we'll use CIM.

Now, here is the twist. Let's start by looking at Win32_BIOS.

```
Get-CimInstance -ClassName Win32_BIOS | Export-Csv -NoTypeInformation -Path
C:\Reports\Win32_Bios.csv.
```

Here is a sample of the CSV fields that were in the CSV output:

```
BiosCharacteristics : System.UInt16[]
BIOSVersion         : System.String[]
ListOfLanguages     : System.String[]
```

So... why is that statement producing those values in the CSV file instead of what is shown to the screen using the `Get-CimInstance -ClassName Win32_BIOS` cmdlet?

Let's look at the members of Win32_BIOS by piping the request to `Get-Member`:

`Get-CimInstance -ClassName Win32_BIOS | Get-Member`

As you can see in Figure 3-10, when looking at the `Get-Member` output, we see those same values listed in the definition of the property members. This means that those values are made up of other multiple parts, or an array of data.

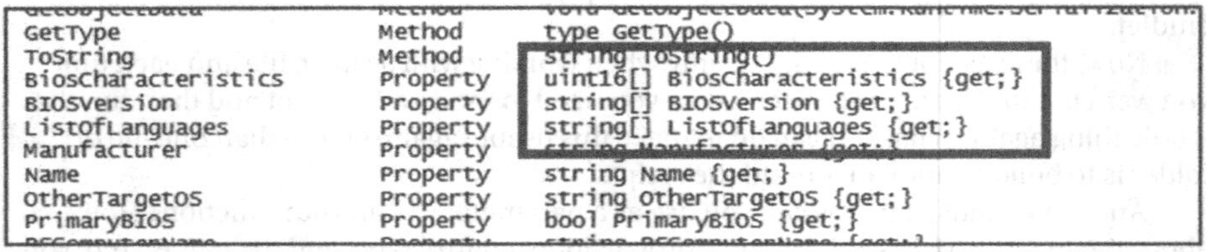

```
GetType              Method     type GetType()
ToString             Method     string ToString()
BiosCharacteristics  Property   uint16[] BiosCharacteristics {get;}
BIOSVersion          Property   string[] BIOSVersion {get;}
ListOfLanguages      Property   string[] ListOfLanguages {get;}
Manufacturer         Property   string Manufacturer {get;}
Name                 Property   string Name {get;}
OtherTargetOS        Property   string OtherTargetOS {get;}
PrimaryBIOS          Property   bool PrimaryBIOS {get;}
```

Figure 3-10. *Sample output of Get-CimInstance -ClassName Win32_BIOS | Get-Member*

Looking at the properties returned from Win32_BIOS, you can see how some of those can have more than one value returned within a single property. However, when outputting that to a flat CSV file, the output does not know how to go from a multi-valued array into a single field. So it is our job to try and massage the data to fitting into a single string value.

Let's just focus on the value of BIOSVersion from the `Win32_BIOS` class, as shown in Figure 3-11.

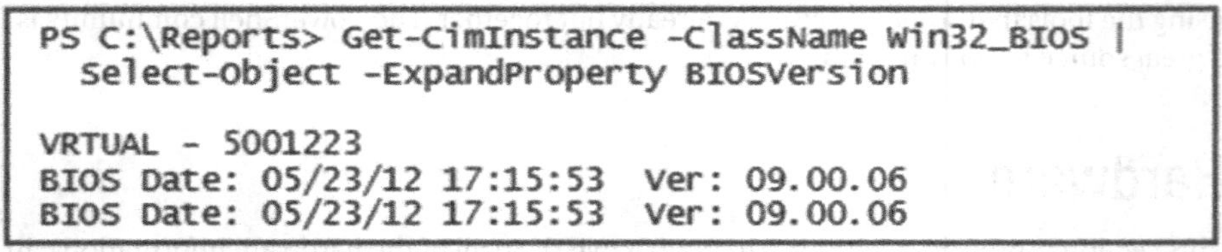

```
PS C:\Reports> Get-CimInstance -ClassName Win32_BIOS |
  Select-Object -ExpandProperty BIOSVersion

VRTUAL - 5001223
BIOS Date: 05/23/12 17:15:53  Ver: 09.00.06
BIOS Date: 05/23/12 17:15:53  Ver: 09.00.06
```

Figure 3-11. *Win32_BIOS BIOSVersion expanded*

In the example, we returned four values that make up the BIOSVersion property, as seen in Figure 3-12, so we will use advanced formatting to make our data from a multivalued array into a single string.

```
PS C:\Reports> Get-CimInstance -ClassName Win32_BIOS |
  Select-Object -Property @{
    Name = 'FormattedBIOSVersion'
    Expression = { $_.BIOSVersion -join ";" }
  } |
  Format-Table -Wrap

FormattedBIOSVersion
--------------------
VRTUAL - 5001223;BIOS Date: 05/23/12 17:15:53  Ver: 09.00.06;BIOS Date: 05/23/12 17:15:53  Ver: 09.00.06
```

Figure 3-12. *Win32_BIOS using advanced formatting*

Let's look at the command used to do this. First, we get the CIM instance Win32_BIOS and pipe that output to the Select-Object cmdlet. Then we use advanced formatting to create a new property called FormattedBIOSVersion and we use an expression to create that value. The expression used first gets the BIOS Version that was piped to it (that's what the $_ tells us) and then we take that value and join the parts of it into a single string with a delimiter of ;. The delimiter could be just about any string or value that makes sense to you.

So if we take the same expression, but export the value to a CSV file, things now work when exporting to a CSV file.

Now, let's reexamine the Win32_BIOS value and make sure that we are collecting only the values that we want to keep.

```
Get-CimInstance -ClassName Win32_BIOS |
  Select-Object -Property Manufacturer,
    SerialNumber,
    ReleaseDate,
    SMBIOSBIOSVersion,
    SMBIOSMajorVersion,
    SMBIOSMinorVersion,
    @{
      Name = 'FormattedBIOSVersion';
      Expression = {$_.BIOSVersion -join ";"}
    }
```

Now we can pipe that information out to a CSV file and the CSV data looks like we expected it to be. This allows us to keep a multivalued property into a flat file, like CSV.

You can also see that we used advanced formatting—a hash table that contains keys such as Name (or Label) and Expression. The value of the expression should be in a script block that returns a result for the current object. Advanced formatting (also known as *calculated property*) allows you to do calculations on objects to produce a new outputs. Advanced formatting can be done within Select-Object or within Format-Table or Format-List.

Computer System Information

Well this section should be shorter because we don't need to explain multivalued arrays being piped to a CSV file. Except, we'll take you to a secret of how we find multivalued property values for most PowerShell cmdlets. The answer is in the Get-Member cmdlet.

For those of you who may not know the Get-Member cmdlet, you should. It is a great PowerShell resource that makes your foo better. We say that the Get-Member cmdlet is the second-most important cmdlet, right behind Get-Help.

So, let's look at the output from the CIM instance for finding computer information. We will use a new cmdlet called Get-CIMClass. As seen in Figure 3-13, this allows us to search for classes that are close to the information that we are looking for.

```
PS C:\Reports> Get-CimClass -Namespace ROOT\CimV2 -ClassName win32*comp*


   NameSpace: ROOT/cimv2

CimClassName                    CimClassMethods    CimClassProperties
------------                    ---------------    ------------------
win32_ComputerSystemEvent       {}                 {SECURITY_DESCRIPTOR, TIME_CREATED, MachineName}
win32_ComputerShutdownEvent     {}                 {SECURITY_DESCRIPTOR, TIME_CREATED, MachineName, Type}
win32_ComputerSystem            {SetPowerState, R... {Caption, Description, InstallDate, Name...}
win32_ComponentCategory         {}                 {Caption, Description, InstallDate, Name...}
win32_ComputerSystemProduct     {}                 {Caption, Description, IdentifyingNumber, Name...}
win32_PublishComponentAction    {Invoke}           {ActionID, Caption, Description, Direction...}
win32_ComputerSystemProcessor   {}                 {GroupComponent, PartComponent}
win32_NTLogEventComputer        {}                 {Computer, Record}
```

Figure 3-13. *Listing classed from CIM*

Wow. Look at all that good stuff that was returned. But because we are only interested in finding computer system information here, let's check the Win32_ComputerSystem, which has information that might be useful.

Again, by using Get-Member we can find values that are returning multiple values for a single property. But this is where a little script might help to determine which properties are single fields and which ones have multiple values returned. Here is the script:

```
# Used to Easily Gather information for a command
# Get the CIM instance for Win32_ComputerSystem
Get-CimInstance -ClassName Win32_ComputerSystem |
  # Now list each property and method of the object
  Get-Member |
  # Just get the properties
  Where-Object MemberType -eq Property |
  # Now loop through each object
  ForEach-Object {
    # Check if the defnintion matches specific strings
    if (($_.Definition -match '\[\]') -or ($_.Definition -match 'collec')) {
      # True - split each part of the property with a ';'
      "@{Name = '$($_.Name)'; Expression = {`$_.$($_.Name) -join ';'} },"
    } else {
      # False - just return the property name
      "$($_.Name),"
    }
}
```

The short version of this script runs a normal PowerShell command, pipes it into Get-Member, and then for each object returned, checks to see if it has a pair of square brackets [ ] or part of the word "collec" used in the definition. If either one of those statements is true, then a long string is displayed; if both of those statements are false, however, then only the Name field for that object is displayed. Now all of this information gets displayed to the current PowerShell session. You need to copy it back into a command to pull the information you want.

And how do you find the specific fields that are important to you? Run the command to list all objects returned from the original command and pipe it to a formatted list, as follows:

```
Get-CimInstance -ClassName Win32_ComputerSystem | Format-List -Property *
```

Did you notice that the output of the previous command has curly brackets { } in it? And, did you notice how the preceding script shows which fields you need to use advanced formatting on to get the data easily saved to a CSV file?

So, examine the fields and choose the values that are good for your environment. In this example, we chose fields important to this example:

```
Get-CimInstance -ClassName Win32_ComputerSystem |
  Select-Object -Property Manufacturer,
    Model,
    DomainRole,
    Domain,
    WorkGroup,
    @{
      Name = 'FormattedRoles';
      Expression = {$_.Roles -join ";"} },
    TotalPhysicalMemory,
    SystemType,
    NumberOfProcessors,
    NumberOfLogicalProcessors,
    DnsHostName,
    CurrentTimeZone
```

Again, running the same command and piping to a CSV file preserves the information for you to check later for changes.

Processor Information

Now things will start sounding familiar. The following explains how you can find information about processors on a computer.

1. Start by listing all classes that match processor.

2. Run the command. Include the Format-List -Property * to show an example of the output.

3. Determine which fields you want to record and examine.

4. Determine if any of those fields have properties that need advanced formatting.

5. Test your command

6. Pipe that information to a CSV file.

Here is a list of the commands:

1. ```
   Get-CimClass -Namespace Root\CimV2 -ClassName win32*processor*
   ```

2. ```
   Get-CimInstance -ClassName Win32_Processor | Format-List
   -Property *
   ```

3. A personal choice, but we like the fields, DeviceID, Status, AddressWidth, MaxClockSpeed, Caption, Description, Name, CurrentClockSpeed

4. None of these fields requires advanced formatting.

5. ```
   Get-CimInstance -ClassName Win32_Processor |
       Select-Object -Property DeviceID,
           Status,
           AddressWidth,
           MaxClockSpeed,
           Caption,
           Description,
           Name,
           CurrentClockSpeed
   ```

6. ```
   Get-CimInstance -ClassName Win32_Processor |
       Select-Object -Property DeviceID,
           Status,
           AddressWidth,
           MaxClockSpeed,
           Caption,
           Description,
           Name,
           CurrentClockSpeed |
       Export-Csv -NoTypeInformation -Path C:\Reports\Win32_Processor.csv
   ```

Now you have learned the commands and the steps to start recording information about a computer. There are several WMI classes that are helpful to record the current state of a server. You have to save all this information. The following is other important information about servers that you may want to check:

- Physical memory

- Operating system

- Storage/Disks

There is a lot of information stored within a computer's Windows Management Instrumentation (WMI). Once you have learned how to glean this information from WMI, you can spend days looking at all of it.

Troubleshooting

In this section, we will explain when you should use WMI versus CIM queries and why they are different. We will also discuss different options required with remote queries while using WMI and CIM cmdlets.

The Difference Between WMI and CIM

What is the difference between WMI and CIM as it pertains to PowerShell?

- WMI: Windows Management Instrumentation uses DCOM, or Distributed COM, which is based on RPC (remote procedure calls).

- CIM: Common Information Model uses WS-MAN, or web services for management, an HTTP-based protocol.

Some older computers do not know how to work with CIM, so you still should know how to use WMI calls.

Firewalls also play a part in which protocol you can or should use. Most larger companies have well-defined protocols that are acceptable for use on the network. You should check with your company if there is a method that may not work in your environment.

Testing in your environment is necessary to determine whether you use WMI or CIM to retrieve information about your computers.

Remote Queries

WMI and CIM sessions can be called against remote computers (they do *not* need to be run locally on each server, as the examples in this chapter show). This allows you to run a script on a single device to connect to other computers in your environment to glean information from each system.

But wait—what about credentials? You may or may not have different credentials for different systems. You need to pass credentials to remote computers in order to query. A simple Get-WMIObject allows you to specify credentials.

Well, let's be glad that is solved ... and yet it isn't. There is no credential option used for Get-CIMInstance.

What?

So what was Microsoft thinking?

The answer is really great. On the newer operating systems that support CIM, Microsoft wants you to create a CIMSession before you connect to a remote computer.

Why would you want to do that?

You probably have to do multiple calls to a remote computer. You don't normally just ask a single question and you're done; you ask more than one question.

In WMI, you have to open a connection to the remote server, pass it credentials, ask your single question, and then tear down the connection to the remote server. The same things are needed for each remote query being used by WMI.

Using CIM, you first create a New-CIMSession and assign that session to the variable. You can pass credentials in that cmdlet; pass-thru credentials are also OK. Once you have created the session, ask as many questions as you need to the remote computer using the session variable. Each query is faster than its WMI counterpart because it has already established a remote session. Once you are done with the remote computer, you can use Remove-CIMSession to tear down the connection to it.

Here is a short example of a CIM session:

```
$computerName = 'Server01'
$cred = Get-Credential
$remoteSession = New-CimSession -ComputerName $computerName -Credential $cred
Get-CimInstance -CimSession $remoteSession -ClassName Win32_LogicalDisk
Get-CimInstance -CimSession $remoteSession -ClassName Win32_BIOS
Get-CimInstance -CimSession $remoteSession -ClassName Win32_ComputerSystem
Get-CimInstance -CimSession $remoteSession -ClassName Win32_Processor
Get-CimInstance -CimSession $remoteSession -ClassName Win32_Memory
Get-CimInstance -CimSession $remoteSession -ClassName Win32_OperatingSystem
Remove-CimSession -CimSession $remoteSession
```

That is a lot faster than having to re-establish a connection to the remote server for each call using WMI.

Next Steps

In this chapter, we discussed how to get information but there is a lot we can do to improve on the examples shown. Start by building a function around one of the cmdlets. The function should include parameters like optional credentials, computer names, and output types.

The function should assume pass-thru credentials, unless you specify to connect to remote computers as another user. The default computer name should be itself, but the option should be to allow it to connect to a remote computer, or lots of remote computers. At times, you won't necessarily want to save all this data as a CSV file each time you run the command; sometimes you may want to display to the console window and not save the data.

Each function should do one thing and do it well. Once you build a few of these functions, you can combine them into a module where common functions are grouped into the same module.

Summary

Documenting your servers is an important step in troubleshooting. It may seem like a lot of work to document your servers, but it really is helpful when you are trying to figure out what changed when a server is not performing as expected. Making sure that you know what changed and how to check for those changes should be an exercise that you practice often and efficiently. There is a lot of information to be gleaned from your servers, but when a server is already broken, that is not the time to start figuring out what changed if you have nothing to base it on.

CHAPTER 4

Installed Applications

This chapter covers applications installed on a system. Getting this information is helpful for documentation and record keeping. It isn't something that you would probably check in the heat of battle during an immediate problem, but knowing how to document what your server is doing is a skill you should learn.

The question is always, "What changed?" It's nice to be able to list the applications on a server, and then compare that list to applications that were installed on the server six months ago. Depending on the change management process in your environment, this should be well documented; however, we have found that most companies need to document what is currently installed on a server. This chapter covers how to discover what is installed on your servers.

■ **Note** There are several ways to gather information about what programs are currently installed. And there is also a very big caveat associated with this: the record of applications installed on your computer depends on the information published by the software manufacturer. That means, for example, if you created a program called TheSilentProgram, you have to register the program in the "normal" locations within the Microsoft operating system. If you don't register your program with the operating system, others may not know that your program was installed. Think about it: viruses do not register themselves on your computer, so it's up to the manufacturer to register the program with the operating system.

Obtaining a List of Installed Applications

There are several places to get a list of applications that are installed on the computer. We will cover two major methods to get a list of installed applications: using CIM and checking the registry.

© Derek Schauland, Donald Jacobs 2016
D. Schauland and D. Jacobs, *Troubleshooting Windows Server with PowerShell*,
DOI 10.1007/978-1-4842-1851-8_4

Using the CIM Object

So let's talk about the option that isn't recommended on production systems. A simple query can look at three random applications may look like what's shown in Figure 4-1.

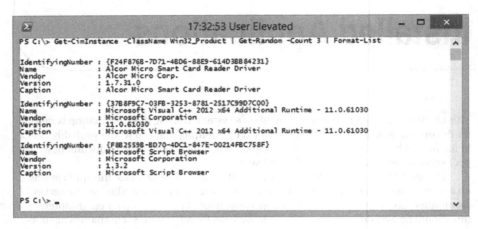

```
                                17:32:53 User Elevated                    _  □  ×
PS C:\> Get-CimInstance -ClassName Win32_Product | Get-Random -Count 3 | Format-List

IdentifyingNumber : {F24F8768-7D71-48D6-88E9-614D3BB84231}
Name              : Alcor Micro Smart Card Reader Driver
Vendor            : Alcor Micro Corp.
Version           : 1.7.31.0
Caption           : Alcor Micro Smart Card Reader Driver

IdentifyingNumber : {3788F9C7-03FB-3253-8781-2517C99D7C00}
Name              : Microsoft Visual C++ 2012 x64 Additional Runtime - 11.0.61030
Vendor            : Microsoft Corporation
Version           : 11.0.61030
Caption           : Microsoft Visual C++ 2012 x64 Additional Runtime - 11.0.61030

IdentifyingNumber : {F8B2559B-BD70-4DC1-847E-00214FBC758F}
Name              : Microsoft Script Browser
Vendor            : Microsoft Corporation
Version           : 1.3.2
Caption           : Microsoft Script Browser


PS C:\> _
```

Figure 4-1. *Getting CIM instances*

■ **Note**   There is a CIM object that queries products, but there is an issue with that query. Paraphrasing from https://support.microsoft.com/en-us/kb/974524, "Win32_product Class is not query optimized. Queries require WMI to use the MSI provider to enumerate all of the installed products and then parse the full list sequentially. This process also initiates a consistency check of packages installed, verifying and repairing the install. With an account with only user privileges, as the user account may not have access to quite a few locations, may cause delay in application launch and an event 11708 stating an installation failure."

What does that mean to production systems? Be careful, because it may cause some applications to reinstall. Hopefully not, but it may reinstall some applications. For this reason, only run this when you have a window of opportunity for downtime.

There are lots or properties associated with the results, but by default, only five are returned, as seen in Figure 4-1. To see a list of all the properties and methods for the Get-CimInstance cmdlet, pipe the cmdlet to the Get-Member cmdlet, as shown in Figure 4-2.

```
┌──────────────────────────── 17:34:20 User Elevated ──────── _ □ × ─┐
│ PS C:\> Get-CimInstance -ClassName Win32_Product | Get-Random -Count 1 | Get-Member   ^ │
│                                                                                         │
│    TypeName: Microsoft.Management.Infrastructure.CimInstance#root/cimv2/Win32_Product   │
│                                                                                         │
│ Name                        MemberType   Definition                                     │
│ ----                        ----------   ----------                                     │
│ Clone                       Method       System.Object ICloneable.Clone()              │
│ Dispose                     Method       void Dispose(), void IDisposable.Dispose()    │
│ Equals                      Method       bool Equals(System.Object obj)                │
│ GetCimSessionComputerName   Method       string GetCimSessionComputerName()            │
│ GetCimSessionInstanceId     Method       guid GetCimSessionInstanceId()                │
│ GetHashCode                 Method       int GetHashCode()                             │
│ GetObjectData               Method       void GetObjectData(System.Runtime.Serialization.Serializat... │
│ GetType                     Method       type GetType()                               │
│ ToString                    Method       string ToString()                            │
│ AssignmentType              Property     uint16 AssignmentType {get;}                 │
│ Caption                     Property     string Caption {get;}                        │
│ Description                 Property     string Description {get;}                     │
│ HelpLink                    Property     string HelpLink {get;}                        │
│ HelpTelephone               Property     string HelpTelephone {get;}                  │
│ IdentifyingNumber           Property     string IdentifyingNumber {get;}              │
│ InstallDate                 Property     string InstallDate {get;}                     │
│ InstallDate2                Property     CimInstance#DateTime InstallDate2 {get;}      │
│ InstallLocation             Property     string InstallLocation {get;}                 │
│ InstallSource               Property     string InstallSource {get;}                   │
│ InstallState                Property     int16 InstallState {get;}                     │
│ Language                    Property     string Language {get;}                        │
│ LocalPackage                Property     string LocalPackage {get;}                    │
│ Name                        Property     string Name {get;}                            │
│ PackageCache                Property     string PackageCache {get;}                    │
│ PackageCode                 Property     string PackageCode {get;}                     │
│ PackageName                 Property     string PackageName {get;}                     │
│ ProductID                   Property     string ProductID {get;}                       │
│ PSComputerName              Property     string PSComputerName {get;}                  │
│ RegCompany                  Property     string RegCompany {get;}                      │
│ RegOwner                    Property     string RegOwner {get;}                        │
│ SKUNumber                   Property     string SKUNumber {get;}                       │
│ Transforms                  Property     string Transforms {get;}                      │
│ URLInfoAbout                Property     string URLInfoAbout {get;}                     │
│ URLUpdateInfo               Property     string URLUpdateInfo {get;}                    │
│ Vendor                      Property     string Vendor {get;}                          │
│ Version                     Property     string Version {get;}                          │
│ WordCount                   Property     uint32 WordCount {get;}                        │
│ PSStatus                    PropertySet  PSStatus {Name, Version, InstallState}        │
└─────────────────────────────────────────────────────────────────────────────────────┘
```

Figure 4-2. *CimInstance Members*

Lots of good information to glean here; however, too much to look at, so let's save everything to a CSV file (see Figure 4-3).

```
┌──────────────────────────── 17:38:33 User Elevated ──────── _ □ × ─┐
│ PS C:\> Get-CimInstance -ClassName Win32_Product | Export-Csv -NoTypeInformation -Path C:\Reports\Ap ^ │
│ psFromWMI_20150409.CSV                                                                   │
│ PS C:\>                                                                                  │
└─────────────────────────────────────────────────────────────────────────────────────┘
```

Figure 4-3. *Exporting CimInstance to CSV*

Now that is fine, but the real question is what is installed today compared to what was installed the last time you looked at the applications.

For that, we can use the Compare-Object cmdlet. We still need to create a current list of installed applications from today and compare that to an earlier export. So for this example, let's use two files: AppsFromWMI_20150109.CSV and AppsFromWMI_20150409.CSV.

■ **Note**   The naming standards that we use are as follows: the file name, an underscore, the date the file was created—YYYYMMDD, and finally, the extension.

So now, before we talk about the script, we need to discuss a few options that could happen while comparing applications from different dates.

- A new application could be installed.

- An application could have been removed.

- An application could have a different version.

So, let's plan what we want the script to do...

1. Get the old file and put it into a variable.

2. Get the new file and put it into a variable.

3. Compare the old file data with the new file data.

4. Check for apps that are new.

5. Check for apps that are old.

6. Check for changes in the file version.

Now, let's look at the code.

This gets the old file and brings it into memory:

```
$OldFile = 'C:\Reports\AppsFromWMI_20150109.CSV'
$OldFileData = Import-Csv -Path $OldFile
$OldIdNumber = $OldFileData | Sort-Object -Property 'IdentifyingNumber' |
    Select-Object -ExpandProperty 'IdentifyingNumber'
```

One of the things that we are also doing here is getting a list of the IdentifyingNumber for each application to compare against the new list of apps. We're sorting the values to put into the Compare-Object cmdlet.

This gets the new file and brings it into memory:

```
$NewFile = 'C:\reports\AppsFromWMI_20150409.CSV'
$NewFileData = Import-Csv -Path $NewFile
$NewIdNumber = $NewFileData | Sort-Object -Property 'IdentifyingNumber' |
    Select-Object -ExpandProperty 'IdentifyingNumber'
```

Again, we extract the IdentifyingNumber for a quick comparison. We only want to compare (for the moment) what is different.

```
$NewOrRemovedAppIds = Compare-Object -ReferenceObject $OldIdNumber `
    -DifferenceObject $NewIdNumber -IncludeEqual
$NewAppIds = $NewOrRemovedAppIds | Where-Object SideIndicator -EQ '=>'
$RemovedAppIds = $NewOrRemovedAppIds | Where-Object SideIndicator -EQ '<='
```

Notice how we are comparing the IdentifyingNumber of the old and new files. We save those to a variable so that we can use the data for later checks. We extract things that are in the new list by checking for the SideIndicator and then extract the removed applications by doing a similar check.

Let's look for new apps that were added since last we checked.

```
$AllNewApps = @()
foreach ($newApp in $NewAppIds) {
    $AllNewApps += $NewFileData |
        Where-Object 'IdentifyingNumber' -EQ $newApp.InputObject
}
Write-Host "`nRecently Installed Applications" -ForegroundColor Yellow
$AllNewApps |
    Select-Object -Property Name, Version, Caption | Format-Table -AutoSize
```

We create an empty array to save data to, and then add all the information from the NewFileData variable from all the NewAppIds. We then only choose certain fields to display to make a nice clean table.

Let's check for apps that have been uninstalled.

```
$AllRemovedApps = @()
foreach ($oldApp in $RemovedAppIds) {
    $AllRemovedApps += $OldFileData |
        Where-Object 'IdentifyingNumber' -EQ $OldApp.InputObject
}
Write-Host "`nRemoved Applications" -ForegroundColor Yellow
$AllRemovedApps |
    Select-Object -Property Name, Version, Caption | Format-Table -AutoSize
```

Using the same logic, let's now check for removed apps.

Check for changed file versions.

```
Write-Host "`nChecking for Changed File Versions" -ForegroundColor Yellow
foreach ($line in $OldFileData) {
    $SameApp = $NewFileData |
        Where-Object 'IdentifyingNumber' -EQ $line.IdentifyingNumber

    # Let's check if the versions match
    if (($SameApp.Version -notmatch $line.Version) -and
    ($SameApp -ne $null)) {
        Write-Host "This software, '$($line.Name)', was updated from version
        '$($line.Version)' to '$($SameApp.Version)'."
    }
}
```

The first thing that we do is get a list of applications that exist in both the old and the new files. However, a side effect of this check is that we might end up with some apps that were removed; so we added a section that can be used for other purposes in your own scripts. We like to do that for testing purposes, so we left it in the script. The other thing we put in there is the check against file versions; if the versions do not match, we simply write a message to the console.

Again, this script is just a sample and starting point for you to improve upon as you discover things in your environment.

Using the Registry Keys

If only things were standard. It would be nice if all vendors followed a standard on "how to install software" and "how to register software." But not all software vendors follow the same standards and not all software vendors even register their software.

Let's start with the major registry keys for installed programs.

- HKLM\Software\Microsoft\Windows\CurrentVersion\Uninstall

- HKLM\Software\Wow6432Node\Microsoft\Windows\ CurrentVersion\Uninstall

- HKU\<User SID>\Software\Microsoft\Windows\CurrentVersion\ Uninstall

- HKU\<User SID>\Software\Microsoft\Installer\Products

- HKLM\Software\Classes\Installer\Products

Software can be installed in any of these keys, but there isn't any standard for what is included in these keys. Your best options are to get all information and examine the fields that relate to you and your unique case. But let's look at each part of the script before putting all the parts together.

■ **Note** Because we are looking into different areas of the registry, it is recommended that you back up the keys that you are examining, just in case changes are made and you run these commands with elevated permissions.

The first thing needed is to map a drive to the HKEY_USERS within the registry. By setting the value of Null equal to our command, we avoid getting output to the screen. If the mapped drive fails, you will still see those messages on the screen; we are only avoiding a success message on the screen.

```
New-PSDrive -Name HKU -PSProvider Registry -Root Registry::HKEY_USERS
```

Next, we go back and review the registry locations of where the programs are registered. Simply create an array to store the values populating the array with additional information as we go along.

```
$softwareKeys = @('HKLM:\SOFTWARE\Microsoft\Windows\CurrentVersion\
Uninstall\',
    'HKLM:\SOFTWARE\Wow6432Node\Microsoft\Windows\CurrentVersion\
    Uninstall\',
    'HKLM:\SOFTWARE\Classes\Installer\Products\'
)
```

Then we need to look at programs registered for individual users on the computers. This is going to require validating the data returned to grab user SIDs. Let's use RegEx to return the SIDs, and then filter out other information.

```
$allLocalUsers = Get-ChildItem -Path HKU: |
    where {$_.Name -match 'S-\d-\d+-(\d+-){1,14}\d+$' } |
    Select-Object -ExpandProperty PSChildName
```

Next, we loop through the array, adding the keys that are unique for each user.

```
foreach ($LU in $allLocalUsers) {
    $softwareKeys += "HKU:\$LU\SOFTWARE\Microsoft\Windows\CurrentVersion\
    Uninstall\"
    $softwareKeys += "HKU:\$LU\SOFTWARE\Microsoft\Installer\Products\"
}
```

Now this is a list of the most common locations to find programs in the registry. Let's find the programs listed in each of the software keys. We will store it in an array called allPrograms. The first thing to do is create an empty array and then add each program to the array.

```
$allPrograms = @()
foreach ($regKey in $softwareKeys) {
    $allPrograms += Get-ChildItem -Path $regKey
}
```

Next, we examine each program and get the details that are returned with each key. For each key, the complete list of properties needs to be examined. This is due to a limitation of PowerShell, which we'll discuss after you examine the code.

In the first part of this loop, we need change the relative path of each program to use a path that in the list of mapped drives. We do that by replacing HKEY_LOCAL_MACHINE with HKLM and HKEY_USERS with HKU. By default, PowerShell has a mapped drive to the HKLM already, which is why we didn't need to map that drive at the beginning of the script.

```
$allDetails = @()
$itemHeaders = @()
foreach ($regItem in $allPrograms) {
    # replace Full Path with Relative Path
    $relPath = ($regItem.Name -replace 'HKEY_LOCAL_MACHINE','HKLM:')
    -replace 'HKEY_USERS','HKU:'
    $allDetails += Get-ItemProperty -Path $relPath
    $itemHeaders += Get-ItemProperty -Path $relPath |
        Get-Member -MemberType Properties -ErrorAction SilentlyContinue |
        Select-Object -ExpandProperty Name
}
```

The $itemHeaders variable contains duplicates without any order; the following code returns only those items in the array that are unique.

```
$FullListOfHeaders = $itemHeaders | Select-Object -Unique | Sort-Object
```

Now, we can save that data to CSV file using all the information that we have gathered so far.

```
$allDetails |
    Select-Object -Property $FullListOfHeaders -ErrorAction SilentlyContinue |
    Export-Csv -NoTypeInformation -Path C:\Reports\InstalledAppsRegistry.csv
```

This takes the allDetails variable, uses all possible headers for all objects in the array, and then pipes that to a CSV file. If you open that file, you can see there are a lot of empty fields, but that's because the uniqueness of each key.

Arrays

According to the help file associated with about_Arrays, Microsoft defines an array as "...a data structure that is designed to store a collection of items. The items can be the same type or different types."

Piping an array to Format-List shows each item in the array with the value for each object. When formatting a list, each object is processed as an individual item, so it shows the properties for each object. When you pipe an array to other formatting choices or output objects, it is assumed that each object has the same properties as the first object sent.

Let's take a look at a simple script to test this.

```
$A = @()
$A += Get-Process | Get-Random -Count 1 | Select-Object Name, Id,
VirtualMemorySize
$A += Get-Service | Get-Random -Count 1
```

So, we created an empty array and added a random process to it only selecting three properties: Name, Id, and VirtualMemorySize. We then grab a random service and add that to the array. Again, not the best choice for an array, but it serves the purpose of this example.

Let's do some testing with this variable.

```
$A | Select-Object -Property * | Format-List
```

Perfect. Each object is exactly what we want to see. Even examining each object for its members produces the data for each object individually. As seen in Figure 4-4, the members of each object in the array are completely different.

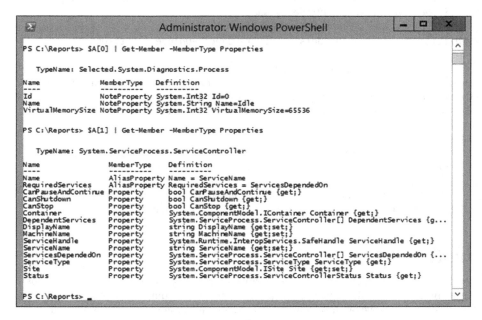

Figure 4-4. *Comparing disparate object members in an array*

However, when we try piping the variable A to a table, only the three properties are shown; it does not display the other fields that were included in the second object.

Piping that to a CSV file produces the same results as the table. Both assume that each object will have the same properties as the first object, so just produce the results using the properties of the first object.

```
$A | Select-Object -Property * | Format-Table
$A | Select-Object -Property * | Export-Csv -Path C:\Reports\Test.csv
```

In order to get around the limitations, we have to tell the next object in the pipeline which headers it will use for the output. Using the simple example again, we'll add some fields to get a complete list of properties, like this:

```
$A = @()
$headers = @()
$A += Get-Process | Get-Random -Count 1 | Select-Object Name, Id,
VirtualMemorySize
$headers += "Name", "ID", "VirtualMemorySize"
$A += Get-Service | Get-Random -Count 1
$headers += Get-Service | Get-Random -Count 1 |
    Get-Member -MemberType Properties -ErrorAction SilentlyContinue |
    Select-Object -ExpandProperty Name

$FullListOfHeaders = $headers | Select-Object -Unique | Sort-Object
```

This time, we added the headers to a new variable and we'll use that later. If you examine the headers variable, you can see that one of the values, Name, exists twice. So we clean that up by getting unique items and sorting them.

Now we can save that to a CSV file by selecting all headers and saving that.

```
$A |
    Select-Object -Property $FullListOfHeaders -ErrorAction SilentlyContinue |
    Export-Csv -NoTypeInformation -Path C:\Reports\ArrayTest.csv
```

We like the speed of how PowerShell handles arrays, but sometimes we want to see all the headers for all the objects piped throughout the commands.

Next Steps

Putting it all together, create a script (or scripts) on creating lists of installed applications. Using both WMI and the registry to get a list of programs is your best chance to document applications. Improve on the examples with verbose messaging, progress meters, and using Try-Catch blocks.

The array portion of getting headers can be done more efficiently by examining all the data once it has been collected; for example, something like this:

```
$headers = @()
foreach ($item in $A) {
    $headers += $item |
        Get-Member -MemberType Properties -ErrorAction SilentlyContinue |
        Select-Object -ExpandProperty Name
}
$FullListOfHeaders = $headers | Select-Object -Unique | Sort-Object
```

Summary

Installed applications are as unique as fingerprints. Where the data gets recorded can differ and which values are added to property fields can vary by manufacturer. We can get applications through a WMI or a CIM call, and we can extract installed applications from the registry. Trying to save an array with different types of data for each object can be tricky, but as you can see, easily done.

CHAPTER 5

■ ■ ■

Windows Update

Windows Update allows operating system files to fix known issues from Microsoft. Originally, it focused only on the operating system, but it now supports all Microsoft products. Windows Update can be installed automatically from the Internet, from onsite Windows Server Update Services, or manually from an offline source.

Windows Update needs to be applied to keep systems up to date. In short, Windows Update prevents problems. We have seen a lot of companies that have stopped applying Windows Update because "reboots and patches break more than they fix." While it is true that occasionally patches do cause trouble, you should still apply patches to prevent future problems.

There are several categories in Windows Update, including the following:

- Critical updates

- Definition updates

- Drivers

- Feature packs

- Security updates

- Service packs

- Tools

- Update rollups

- Updates

This chapter focuses on collecting information from on a computer with a currently installed Windows Update. We will find installed updates and information about those updates. We briefly discuss options for creating scripts that find and install Windows Update from the command line, but only do this to demonstrate that it can be done. Lastly, we briefly discuss removing patches from a computer if a problem should arise.

© Derek Schauland, Donald Jacobs 2016
D. Schauland and D. Jacobs, *Troubleshooting Windows Server with PowerShell*,
DOI 10.1007/978-1-4842-1851-8_5

Get-HotFix

Get-HotFix is a great command because you can run it locally or remotely. As long as you have administrative permissions on a remote computer, you can poll remote computers to find their history of installed hotfixes. Looking at the help for Get-HotFix, shown in Figure 5-1, you can see that there is not much to it, but it returns powerful information.

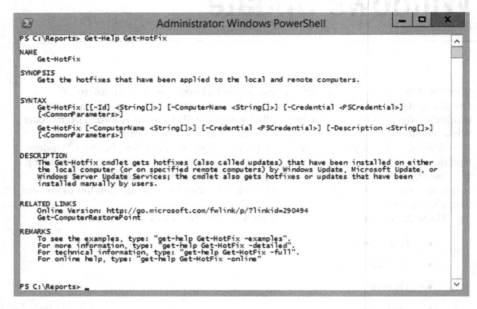

Figure 5-1. *Get-Help Get-HotFix*

As you can see, updates can be listed on the local computer (default) or on other computers, and it accepts the use of alternate credentials.

Scenario

You get a call that an application server has stopped processing requests. According to everyone who has looked at the server before you, nothing has changed.

Resolution

One of the first things that we consider is what was installed recently. We usually start with Windows Update to determine this by running a quick command, like this:

```
Get-HotFix -ComputerName server01 | Sort-Object InstalledOn
```

And voilà! You see that a set of hotfixes were just installed on the computer. Then it is a matter of the following other quick checks:

- Was the server recently rebooted?

- Is the computer pending a reboot?

- Are all the required services running?

Using WMI or CIM

If you prefer to use WMI or CIM to query, you can also look for hotfixes with the Win32_QuickFixEngineering class. WMI and CIM return the same information as the cmdlet, Get-HotFix, which uses the Win32_QuickFixEngineering WMI class. There are situations where you may need to use one or the other, so be sure that you are aware of this option. We won't be covering it much more in this chapter.

Details of Get-HotFix Results

Let's look at the detailed list of items returned from a random hotfix. As you can see, there is a lot of information returned. The following are the key fields:

- InstalledOn: Shows when the hotfix was installed.

- InstalledBy: Shows who did the patching; sometimes it is NT Authority\System, which means that the computer itself installed the update.

- HotFixID: The hotfix id number. It shows which updates were applied.

- Caption: Usually the URL that is associated with the hotfix.

- Description: Describes what kind of update was installed.

The help output for Get-HotFix is displayed in Figure 5-2.

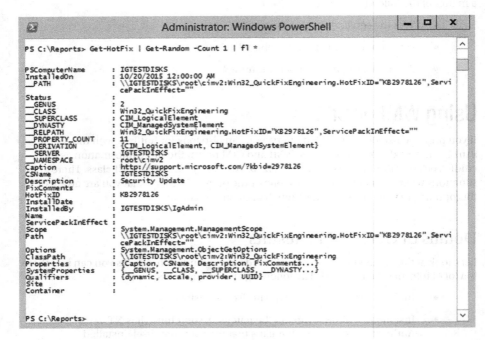

Figure 5-2. *Details of a Hotfix*

Customizing this Code

We can save this as a script and then add lots of bells and whistles. We can also add a parameter section so that we can change the computer name as needed, or even change the parameter to accept multiple computer names. Instead of just saying to the screen that the computer is pending a reboot, you can perform actions on the remote computer, such as rebooting, if it is required.

Checking When a Computer Was Rebooted

Each time that the computer starts, it is recorded into the computer; it is just a matter of reading that value and putting it into human-readable form. Let's look at the command to pull the start time of the computer and put into human-readable form.

```
[Management.ManagementDateTimeConverter]::ToDateTime((Get-WmiObject
Win32_OperatingSystem -ComputerName $env:ComputerName -ErrorAction Stop).
LastBootUpTime)
```

Now, something like that makes it hard to remember and hard for other computers to change, so let's make it easier to read.

```
$ComputerName = "$env:ComputerName"
$operatingSystem = Get-WmiObject Win32_OperatingSystem -ComputerName
$ComputerName
```

As you can see, we connected to another computer using WMI and returned the Win32_OperatingSystem class. Once we have that, we can look at all the note properties of that variable.

```
$operatingSystem | Get-Member
```

Examining the list of properties, you can see that there is one called LastBootUpTime. That's simple enough. The output of these commands is shown in Figure 5-3.

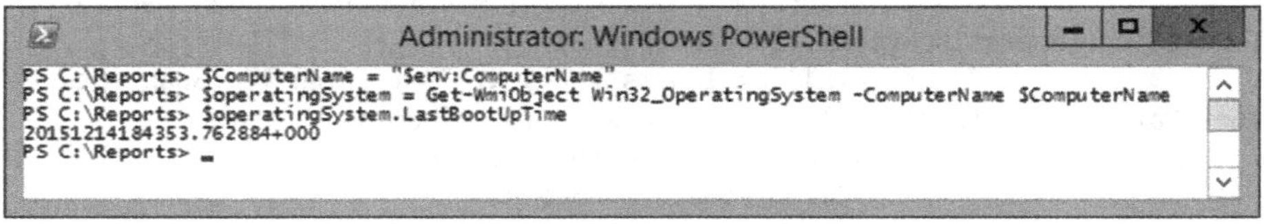

Figure 5-3. *LastBootUpTime's not so friendly output*

But wait, why does the result look like that? That's because WMI has a few date-time formats. Finding the correct conversion is usually trial and error. Since we have tried and failed, the conversion will use another class, called ManagementDateTimeConverter. Moving in and out of these formats often involves messy parsing code. Luckily, the WMI team was nice enough to make sure that the .NET classes you use to work with WMI can convert dates, times, and timespans.

So, we can use this class to convert that to a readable format:

```
[Management.ManagementDateTimeConverter]::ToDateTime($operatingSystem.
LastBootUpTime)
```

Examining the data reveals when the server was last booted, and based on the information, it is very easy to determine the uptime of the server.

Improvements to this Code

You can turn this into a function that can be dot sourced or used in your own modules for quick use.

```
Function Get-TsSystemUptime {
    [CmdletBinding(SupportsShouldProcess=$true,
                   ConfirmImpact='Medium')]
```

69

```
    Param (
        # A name of a computer, or computers.
        [string[]]$ComputerName = $env:COMPUTERNAME
    )
    Begin { }
    Process {
        # Sets an empty array for this variable
      $results = @()
        Foreach ($comp in $computerName) {
            # Creates a new PowerShell Object
            $intResults = New-Object PSObject
            Write-Verbose -Message "Checking '$comp'"
            if (Test-Connection -ComputerName $comp -Quiet -Count 2) {
                Try {
                    $operatingSystem = Get-WmiObject Win32_OperatingSystem -
ComputerName $comp -ErrorAction Stop
                    $lastStartTime = [Management.ManagementDateTimeConverter]::
ToDateTime($operatingSystem.LastBootUpTime)
                    [double]$TotalHours = "{0:N2}" -f ((New-TimeSpan -Start
(Get-Date "$lastStartTime") -End (Get-Date)).TotalHours)
                    $intResults = [PSCustomObject]@{
                        'ComputerName' = $comp
                        'LastStartTime' = $lastStartTime
                        'TotalHours' = $TotalHours
                    }
                    $results += $intResults
                }
                Catch {
                    Write-Warning -Message "The computer '$comp' was not
reachable because $_."
                }
            } else {
                Write-Warning -Message "The computer '$comp' was not
pingable."
            }
        }
    }
    End { $results }
}
```

Most of the examples given in this book can be used to create functions and, in turn, create modules.

Uninstalling a Hot Fix

Sometimes you find that you need to uninstall a hotfix. This can be done using a built-in tool called wusa.exe. Information about it is at https://support.microsoft.com/en-us/kb/934307.

PowerShell does not have native tools to uninstall updates, so we can use the wusa.exe inside PowerShell to remove updates.

This simple function runs against a local machine and removes the hotfix.

```
Function Uninstall-TSHotFix {
  [CmdletBinding()]
  Param (
    # This is the HotFix ID, can be either KB plus number or just number.
    [Parameter(Mandatory=$true)]
    $HotFixID
  )
  $HotFixID = $HotFixID -replace 'kb',''
  $FoundHotFix = Get-HotFix | where HotfixID -match $HotFixID
  if ($FoundHotFix) {
    wusa /uninstall /kb:$HotFixID /quiet /norestart
  } else {
    Write-Warning -Message "Cannot find HotFixID '$HotFixID'"
  }
}
```

This script simply checks if the HotFixID parameter is on the local computer and then removes the hotfix.

Improvements to this Function

The wsua.exe tool does not work on remote computers. So, we can use PowerShell to start a remote process on another computer. We also need to verify that the hot fix is on a remote computer. It's a good thing that the Get-HotFix cmdlet and the Win32_QuickFixEngineering WMI class query remote computers.

We can also use PowerShell to start a remote process on another computer.

The following example shows how you can start a remote process.

```
$ComputerName = 'Server01'
$HotFixID = '123456789'
$RemoteProcess = "wusa.exe /uninstall /KB:$HotFixID /quiet /norestart"
([WMICLASS]"\\$ComputerName\ROOT\CIMV2:win32_process").
Create($RemoteProcess)
```

By calling the WMICLASS and using the create method, we can start processes remotely. The string that we are using is in the RemoteProcess variable. You can use just about any string you need, just modify it to suit your individual needs.

We can also monitor the remote processes using the Get-Process cmdlet.

Pending Restarts

The easiest way to check for an application that was installed was to look for a pending restart key in the registry. On the local computer, you can do a quick check for a path like this:

```
Test-Path "HKLM:\SOFTWARE\Microsoft\Windows\CurrentVersion\Component Based Servicing\RebootPending"
```

If this key exists, the computer is waiting for a reboot. If this key doesn't exist, well, you know. (Psst. If you don't know, the answer is without the registry key, no reboot is required.) So how do we verify that the key exists on a remote computer? Let's examine some code to check for a restart.

Looking at a remote computer requires some .NET calls to connect to the remote registry.

```
$ComputerName = "$env:ComputerName"
$connectToRegistry = [Microsoft.Win32.RegistryKey]::OpenRemoteBaseKey("Local Machine", $ComputerName.computername)
```

In this example, we are connecting to the local computer again, but the name can be changed to a remote computer. Once we have done this, we can view the connectToRegistry variable and view its members, as shown in Figure 5-4.

```
$connectToRegistry | Get-Member
```

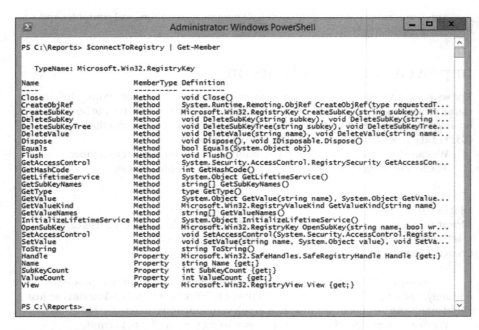

Figure 5-4. *Members of the Remote Registry*

This shows you some of the methods that are available. You can also look up the RegistryKey Class page on MSDN (https://msdn.microsoft.com/en-us/library/microsoft.win32.registrykey.aspx) to see some the methods. The method that we are interested in is the OpenSubKey method. Now connect to the registry that we care about.

```
$fullRegPath = $connectToRegistry.OpenSubKey( "Software\Microsoft\Windows\
CurrentVersion\Component Based Servicing" )
```

Again, we can look at the member of this variable by piping the variable to the Get-Member cmdlet.

```
$fullRegPath | Get-Member
```

Because we are still looking at the remote registry, the methods are the same as before. However, we are going to focus on finding sub key names.

Once we are connected and have the registry path that we care about, we list the subkeys that are under the key.

```
$subKeyNames = $fullRegPath.GetSubKeyNames()
```

Perfect. We now have a list of registry key names that we can examine if there is a pending reboot.

```
if ($subKeyNames -contains 'RebootPending') {Write-Host "$ComputerName Needs
reboot"}
```

There are other things that we can do with networking protocols. Let's close our connection to the remote computer.

```
$fullRegPath.Close()
$connectToRegistry.Close()
```

There are several locations in the registry that need to be checked to find pending restarts. You can use the preceding logic to query and find information in the registry for different types of restarts the computer may be waiting on.

Table 5-1 shows three other locations in the registry that hold information about computer pending restarts.

Table 5-1. *Checking for Computer Restarts*

Component-based services	HKLM\SOFTWARE\Microsoft\Windows\ CurrentVersion\ Component Based Servicing\
Windows Update	HKLM\SOFTWARE\Microsoft\Windows\ CurrentVersion\ WindowsUpdate\Auto Update\
Computer renames	HKLM\SYSTEM\CurrentControlSet\Control\ ComputerName\ ComputerName\ComputerName
Pending file rename	HKLM\SYSTEM\CurrentControlSet\Control\Session Manager\ PendingFileRenameOperations

Summary

Hotfixes can be found by using the Get-HotFix cmdlet or by using WMI/CIM calls to a computer. You can see when updates were applied to a computer. The determination of pending reboots may show if something was installed, but the computer wasn't restarted after the install. And the system uptime shows when a computer was last rebooted.

CHAPTER 6

■ ■ ■

Manage Running Processes on a Target System

So far in our journey to troubleshoot systems using PowerShell, we have gathered information from

- The Windows event log

- Server information

- Installed application listings

- Windows Update information

The information that can be pulled from these sources is large and can quickly be scaled to allow collection from any number of systems. In this chapter, we are going to collect information about processes running on a specified target computer.

What can be captured about processes? Aren't they just objects representing the applications running on a computer?

Processes represent the applications and services actively running on a Windows computer. Some processes can be paused and restarted, all processes can be terminated, and new processes can be started. When this might be useful depends on the situation and what needs to be done.

Working with Processes

Scenario: Suppose there is a server running your company's largest business application and that application is having issues being accessed by the QA administrator for feature testing. The application uses a web browser to access its features, but when the browser is opened, it just disappears. No errors are shown, but nothing is working.

There are a number of ways to look at processes on a computer to see just what they are doing and how many resources they are consuming. Resource overconsumption can also cause things to behave strangely on a Windows system; examining the application's processes can lead you down the right path during the troubleshooting process.

Because we are focusing on PowerShell for troubleshooting, we assume that you have seen the processes tab of the Windows Task Manager before, but it is shown in Figure 6-1.

© Derek Schauland, Donald Jacobs 2016
D. Schauland and D. Jacobs, *Troubleshooting Windows Server with PowerShell*,
DOI 10.1007/978-1-4842-1851-8_6

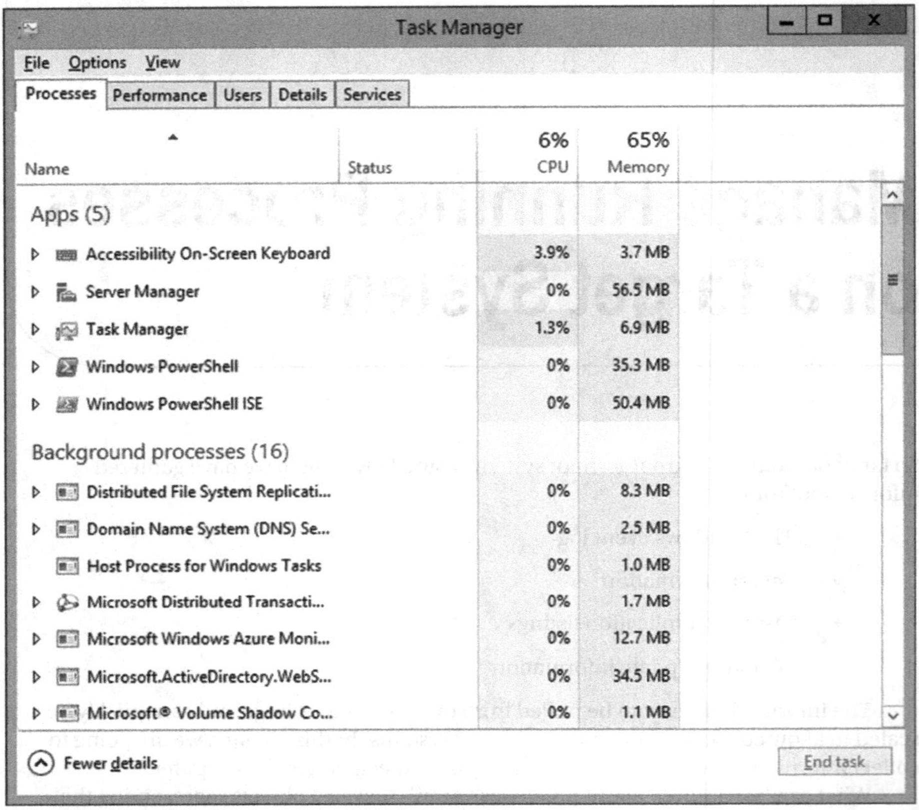

Figure 6-1. *Windows Server 2012R2 Task Manager*

The same information shown there can be returned in the PowerShell console as well. The command to return these results is Get-Process.

Running this cmdlet returns current processes on the local system. On the current system, for example, the process output is shown in Figure 6-2.

```
PS C:\Reports> Get-Process

Handles  NPM(K)    PM(K)      WS(K) VM(M)   CPU(s)     Id ProcessName
-------  ------    -----      ----- -----   ------     -- -----------
    133      10     1656       7356    81     0.08   4920 AtBroker
     56       7     3396       9264    61     0.19   3272 conhost
    221      12     1640       3744    47     0.63    372 csrss
     87       9     1188       3396    42     0.08    436 csrss
    166      14     1900      20560   186     0.78   3508 csrss
    332      31    14632      20504   625     2.11   1284 dfsrs
    145      13     1956       5728    34     0.05   1608 dfssvc
    296      33     6420       8688    48     0.75   1316 dns
    178      14    12336      22164    89     0.08    816 dwm
    199      20    11184      40216   131     0.69   3908 dwm
   1041      54    29124      67900   377     3.41   3304 explorer
      0       0        0          4     0                 0 Idle
    294      21    12904      24224   142     0.28    800 LogonUI
   1467     106    63304      68708  1191    13.27    544 lsass
   1662      39    59076      68336   585     2.78   1212 Microsoft.ActiveDirectory.WebServices
    159      12     2352       6980    41     0.06   1104 msdtc
    186      16     4364      13360   117     0.33   3392 osk
    443      33    74624      83764   662     2.81   4760 powershell
    445      51   109404     130928   880     9.17   5060 powershell_ise
    222      10     1712       6764    84     0.20   3832 rdpclip
    118       9     2484        420    63     0.03   1096 rundll32
    118       9     2684        476    63     0.03   1544 rundll32
    540      44    94496      86784   756     9.41   3164 ServerManager
    262      10     3276       7912    32     2.27    536 services
     55       2      280       1024     4     0.05    264 smss
    365      20     3348       9616    75     0.25   1188 spoolsv
    389      33     8656      13540    58     0.80    528 svchost
    411      14     3836      10308    46     0.69    676 svchost
    376      19     3516       7516    34     1.72    716 svchost
    517      23    13216      18096    72    26.92    848 svchost
   1379      44    17160      31300   135    25.25    872 svchost
    453      26     5344      11248    83     0.77    900 svchost
    662      35     8056      17724  1138     1.22    996 svchost
    344      16     3496      10712    82     0.27   1300 svchost
    731      28    44180      44972   169     2.70   1364 svchost
    102       8     1292       4684    21     0.16   2056 svchost
    265      18     2920       8824    52     0.63   2076 svchost
    378      25     9164      13132   639     4.16   2112 svchost
    809       0      104        284     3    10.27      4 System
    162      11     1612       6528    86     0.09   3160 taskhostex
    274      20    10064      21020   128     2.53   1196 Taskmgr
    160      15     2100       8060    48     0.09   1548 vds
    115       9     1416       5888    39     0.03   2248 VSSVC
    352      37    34800      41536   580     1.52   1368 WaAppAgent
    619      40    34732      47680   576     4.17   1456 WindowsAzureGuestAgent
    433      44    41644      52880   609     4.53   1516 WindowsAzureTelemetryService
     79       8      792       3840    45     0.09    472 wininit
    120       8     1232       5716    56     0.08    464 winlogon
    147       7     1236       5392    50     0.20    824 winlogon
```

Figure 6-2. *Windows Server 2012R2 Process from Get-Process cmdlet*

There is a good amount of information shown by default. The properties shown for each process by default are:

- Handles: The number of handles open by the process

- NPM(K): The amount of non-pageable memory (in KB) used by the process

- PM(K): The amount of pageable memory (in KB) used by the process

- WS(K): The size (in KB) of the working set consumed by the process

- VM(M): The amount of virtual memory (in MB) consumed by the process

- CPU(s): The amount of CPU time (in seconds) consumed by the process

- Id: The numeric identifier of a Windows process

- ProcessName: The name of the running executable

While the Get-Process cmdlet shows this information by default for all processes running on a system, you can manipulate the results in a few ways to drill down to the process in which you are interested.

Filtering by Process ID or Name

Suppose you are working to find out information about a specific process—PowerShell, for example. You can get to PowerShell by running the following one-liner:

```
Get-Process | where Name -eq powershell
```

This shows only the processes with the name "powershell".

■ **Note**   For older versions of PowerShell (prior to version 3), you have to use the legacy version of the Where-Object cmdlet, as shown here:

```
Get-Process | Where-Object {$_.name -eq "powershell"}
```

The $_ is a generic variable used in PowerShell before the release of version 3. In the example, it is used to represent the object that was used before the pipe symbol. For versions 3 and greater, this variable works without any problems.

That same command can also look like this:

```
Get-Process | Where-Object {$PSItem.name -eq "powershell"}
```

The $PSItem was introduced in PowerShell version 3 to make your code easier to read. In both examples, the $_ is the same things as $PSItem, as long as you are running PowerShell version 3 or later.

Most of the time, you will know the name of the application that you are looking for rather than the process ID, and that is perfectly fine. If you need to work with a specific instance of a process because more than one instance is running, you can dig into the details of the processes. You can compare items, for example, when each process started (if you know one started after the other), or maybe the same executable run from different locations on the computer.

Figure 6-3 shows an example of many apps running from different locations, and how you need to choose the correct ID for the process that you want to work with.

```
PS C:\Reports> Get-Process |
>>     where Name -eq GettingSSIDs |
>>     Select-Object Name,
>>         ID,
>>         MainWindowTitle,
>>         StartTime,
>>         Path |
>>     Format-Table -AutoSize
>>

Name           Id MainWindowTitle     StartTime             Path
----           -- ---------------     ---------             ----
GettingSSIDs  532 Finding SSID Information 1/3/2016 7:33:30 AM C:\UAT\GettingSSIDs.exe
GettingSSIDs 1476 Finding SSID Information 1/3/2016 7:30:29 AM C:\Reports\GettingSSIDs.exe
GettingSSIDs 1760 Finding SSID Information 1/3/2016 7:30:49 AM C:\Custom App\GettingSSIDs.exe
GettingSSIDs 4076 Finding SSID Information 1/3/2016 7:33:23 AM C:\DEV\GettingSSIDs.exe


PS C:\Reports> _
```

Figure 6-3. Getting processes and showing specific properties

Here you begin with name-based filtering to narrow down the processes to a certain set of items, and then use the process id (PID) to dig in further to get down to a specific instance.

You can then get the process ID from the previous query with PowerShell. In this case, the ids are 532, 1476, 1760, and 4076. When you run this again for the following process id

```
Get-Process | where ID -eq 4076
```

or in an even shorter syntax, such as

```
- get-process -id 4076
```

you see some of the information tied to that specific process id.

Sorting and Selecting Information Needed

Once information has been returned to the console, you can manipulate it to show the details that are relevant to you. Sometimes information displayed by default is not quite what you need. PowerShell is not holding out on you; there is more to the story and it can be accessed in a few ways.

Listing all of a process's available properties involves using the Select-Object cmdlet.

Pulling in the information about a specific process and piping it to Select-Object does this:

```
Get-Process -ID 4076 | Select-Object -Property *
```

Because we used a process id (4076), the details of that process are pulled out and sent to Select-Object. Once there, the wildcard (*) is used to tell select to return everything. Because there are now more than five properties listed, the results are returned as a list rather than a table. This is shown in Figure 6-4.

```
Administrator: Windows PowerShell                           _  □  X

PS C:\Reports> Get-Process | where ID -eq 4076 | Select-Object *


__NounName                  : Process
Name                        : GettingSSIDs
Handles                     : 246
VM                          : 726433792
WS                          : 90841088
PM                          : 85860352
NPM                         : 39344
Path                        : C:\DEV\GettingSSIDs.exe
Company                     :
CPU                         : 1.90625
FileVersion                 : 1.0.0.1
ProductVersion              : 1,0,0,1
Description                 :
Product                     : GettingSSIDs
Id                          : 4076
PriorityClass               : Normal
HandleCount                 : 246
WorkingSet                  : 90841088
PagedMemorySize             : 85860352
```

Figure 6-4. *The process details for Process ID 4076*

Notice that the output runs off the screen; this is because there are more properties displayed than fit in the confines of the console. This can be modified by filtering the records returned to show only the items specifically needed. As a rule of thumb, working from a large dataset to a smaller dataset works best because this shows you what is available and allows you to filter the result set.

Recall the earlier scenario where the business application was unable to be used when testing but no errors appeared. Now that the Get-Process cmdlet has been used, we can use it to see if there are any issues with the browser used to run the testing.

```
Get-Process -name iexplore
```

This returns all instances of the iexplore.exe process, which runs Internet Explorer. As shown in Figure 6-5, there are five Internet Explorer processes running. Some applications do not behave as expected when an excessive number of processes are running; this may or may not be enough to cause errors on your server, but as an example, it works quite well.

```
Select Administrator: Windows PowerShell                    _  □  X

Handles  NPM(K)    PM(K)    WS(K) VM(M)   CPU(s)     Id ProcessName
-------  ------    -----    ----- -----   ------     -- -----------
    388      29    12424    35328   244     0.28   1688 iexplore
    440      33    16280    34520   242     0.27   1732 iexplore
    386      29    12080    32004   228     0.20   2740 iexplore
    676      71    13068    35032   213     0.80   3208 iexplore
    382      29    11892    27892   224     0.19   4916 iexplore


PS C:\Reports> _
```

Figure 6-5. *Internet Explorer processes running on the local machine*

Working with Returned Data

Returning data about processes is useful at the command line if you know what you are looking for (e.g., information about the PowerShell.exe process) or you are trying to determine how to get to the property or properties that you seek. It may be more useful to create regularly executed reports containing process information to provide a snapshot of what is happening on a system or group of systems.

The process to create a report is similar to that of previous items; the details change based on the information available.

As an example, we can get the processes running at the time the PowerShell script or commands are executed, and then create a report for that data. Since processes change frequently, a timed execution of a PowerShell script to gather the point in time data is recommended.

```
Get-Process | Select-Object -Property Id, Name, WS, CPU
```

This returns the id, name, WorkingSet (WS), and CPU for all the processes currently running on the local computer. From here, we can format the data and output an HTML report to make things a bit easier to read.

```
Get-Process |
  Select-Object -Property Id, Name, WS, CPU |
  ConvertTo-Html -Title "Proccess on $($env:COMPUTERNAME)" |
  Out-File C:\Reports\Processes.html
```

In this code, we are converting our process data to HTML with a page title called "Processes on Computername" (computername as called out in the code snippet would be the name of your computer). This is functional but not very attractive; using more advanced formatting cleans up the output even further. The following code accomplishes this.

```
$header = @"
<style>
BODY{background-color:white;}
TABLE{border-width: 1px;border-style: solid;border-color: black;border-collapse: collapse;}
TH{border-width: 1px;padding: 0px;border-style: solid;border-color: black;}
TD{border-width: 1px;padding-left: 0px;padding-right: 15px;border-style: solid;border-color: black;}
</style>
"@

$serv = Get-Service |
    Select-Object -Property ServiceName, DisplayName, Status |
    Get-Random -Count 7 |
    ConvertTo-Html -Fragment
```

81

```
ConvertTo-Html  -Head $header -body "<H2>Seven Random Services</H2>$serv" |
    Out-File -FilePath "c:\reports\myfile.html"

& C:\Reports\SevenRandomServices.html
```

Delivering the Goods: A Quick Sidestep to Sending Email

Reporting is a handy way to review information generated by PowerShell, but if you had to chase the files down every day, it would be quite tedious. Fortunately, PowerShell provides cmdlets for sending email. This way, anyone who needs to see the reports can get the details on the same schedule.

You need access to an SMTP server to send mail, whereas most servers (including Gmail) require logging in to send mail. An SMTP relay can be used to handle relaying from your internal network to the email server (or service) that your organization uses.

The following is a simple way to send email:

```
Send-MailMessage -To "User@your.company.suffix" `
    -From "reports@your.company.suffix" `
    -Subject 'Report of Processes' `
    -Body "$(Get-Content C:\Reports\SevenRandomServices.html)" `
    -BodyAsHtml `
    -SmtpServer smtp.your.company.suffix
```

You have to modify the values in this example to match your local environments.

■ **Note**   In the preceding example, there is a backtick character at the end of each line, which tells PowerShell that the script line is not over, just starting on the next line. This makes it cleaner to show long lines of code in a more readable format.

So far in this chapter, we have shown you how to gather information from your local computer, and how to produce an HTML report based on that data and send it in an email to anyone interested. This is great if you plan to collect data about this machine, but the real power in getting information comes from remote computers and servers in your environment.

Collecting Information from a Remote Computer or Computers

The Get-Process cmdlet supports the -ComputerName parameter, which allows you to execute the cmdlet and gather information from a specified computer. To work with data for multiple computers, you can provide a comma-separated list or a list of system names in a text file.

For input files, the text file should contain one item per line with no header information. You could also pull in a CSV or XML file if needed, but a plain text file keeps this simple. That is what we used in this example:

```
$inputFile = Get-Content -Path "C:\JustComputerNames.txt"
$reportData = @{}
Foreach ($computer in $inputFile) {
  $reportData += Get-Process -ComputerName $computer
}
$reportData |
  Select-Object -Property MachineName, Id, Name, WS, CPU |
  ConvertTo-Html -Title "Proccesses on Computer List" |
  Out-File C:\Reports\Processes.html

Send-MailMessage -To "User@your.company.suffix" `
  -From "reports@your.company.suffix" `
  -Subject 'Report of Processes' `
  -Body "List of Processes on the computer list." `
  -BodyAsHtml `
  -Attachments 'C:\Reports\Processes.html' `
  -SmtpServer smtp.your.company.suffix
```

Now we have a script that gets process information from specified computers and emails it to the administrator as an HTML file attachment. This is great to get started. It helps you understand execution and how things in PowerShell are run. But it can be further amplified using the scheduled task application in Windows. This way, the script is executed on a schedule; for example, every day at 3:00AM, the email and report file are waiting for the recipient when they arrive to work.

Other Ways to Improve the Script

The following are ways to improve the script.

- Verify that the list of computers in the text file actually exists. Too many times, the source files get moved or modified and so the script stops working. A simple Try-Catch to verify the file was found works, as long as the Catch block does more than just output data to the screen, which isn't helpful when run as a scheduled task.

- You should never assume that the list of computers in the text file are accurate. Wrapping the Get-Process cmdlet inside a Try-Catch block assures that the computer is available. If it isn't, the Catch block should be notifying you about the failure.

- Adding formatting to the HTML code would be nice. This version of the HTML code is dry and not easy to read. Perhaps adding a section for each computer in the report or formatting every other line with color would make it easier to read.

- Saving the file each day with the same name destroys historical data. You may want to incorporate the date the file was saved into the name of the file.

Starting and Stopping Processes

Looking at process information for a system (or group of systems) is great, but it doesn't really get you much, other than a point-in-time look at what things are running on a system when the command is executed. If you run Get-Process on your computer and see that Word.exe is running, then run the same command again after closing Word; it will show that Word.exe is no longer running.

If, however, you find that there is a process causing a computer to perform poorly or is using up all available memory, PowerShell can help.

Suppose that Word.exe is causing a computer to perform at less than optimal levels, or at first glance, it seems that when using Word, things get slow and the computer becomes almost unusable.

The Get-Process cmdlet in PowerShell shows the processes that are running and how much of the available resources each process is consuming. Generally, the problem process isn't going to be Word.exe, but any process will work for this example.

If Word is running away with all of the memory in the system and it needs to be stopped, PowerShell has a way to allow you (as the administrator) to stop most processes that you can see.

Heading back to the example with Word.exe, you can run something like this:

```
Get-Process | where name –EQ word
```

Notice that the command did not return any values. This is because the name of the process isn't Word, but Winword.exe. Appending the preceding statement to account for this will get the process that we were looking for, as follows:

```
Get-Process | where name –match word
```

Using the match operator, the cmdlet found the Winword.exe process. For this session, it produced the following information:

```
Handles NPM(K)  PM(K)  WS(K) VM(M) CPU(s)   Id ProcessName
------- ------  -----  ----- ----- ------   -- -----------
   1099     52  77424  87332 33473   2.98 3032 WINWORD
   1403     73 141196 188288 33596  18.69 7744 WINWORD
```

We can see that the first process is currently using 77424K of private memory and the second process is using 141196K of private memory.

If we wanted to end this process because it was causing unnecessary performance problems, we could simply return to the previous line of code and pipe that to another cmdlet called Stop-Process.

Let's pipe to the Stop-Process cmdlet to the end of the line.

```
Get-Process | where name -match word | Stop-Process
```

This stops both Winword.exe processes from running and forcibly closes both Word applications. However, be careful when closing applications this way; it may cause data loss within that application.

In addition to ending processes, you can also start them within PowerShell. In the last example, we ended the Winword.exe process. Here we start an instance of Microsoft Word.

Going back one more time to our earlier scenario with the non-working line of business application, we were at the point where we found five instances of Internet Explorer running. Using a command similar to the one just discussed, we can end all of the potentially problematic instances of IE by executing the following:

```
Get-Process | where Name -EQ iexplore | Stop-Process
```

Once these processes are stopped, starting a completely new instance without any overhead may help with troubleshooting.

Use the Start-Process cmdlet and then the name of the executable to run, as follows:

```
Start-Process winword
```

This launches an instance of Word. It works as long as the name of the executable you want to start lives in the App Paths registry key. If the registry subkey for Winword does not exist there, then the Winword executable must be in the environmental variable for "path". If you want to start a process that is not listed in the App Paths registry keys or in the path environmental variable, you have to give the full path to the executable.

When Start-Process and Stop-Process Are Useful

Most times, opening and closing the application using the native GUI (graphical user interface) tools is just fine. After all, app programmers ask if you want to save your progress or they do other checks when you close an application. However, there are some instances on your local machine when you may want to start or end processes from PowerShell. For example, when an application becomes unresponsive or the GUI freezes up, you may find that closing an application through PowerShell is the only way to end some processes.

Remember to pay close attention to the processes you are stopping from PowerShell because stopping the wrong one may produce unintended consequences.

Select First, Then Again, and Then Stop

This is much like the adage "measure twice, cut once" to ensure that you are going to get exactly what you expect. If you run a command and immediately pipe it to another cmdlet that takes action, the results may not be what you expect. In this case, and in almost any case where the last cmdlet does something to the input, getting the information a few times to ensure that the results are what you need never hurt anyone.

Using the Invoke-Command cmdlet with -ComputerName and -ScriptBlock parameters is a way to run these cmdlets on a remote computer. This connects to the remote computer and then executes the scriptblock provided. This method is useful when the cmdlets you need to execute do not directly support the –ComputerName parameter.

The following is an example of this:

```
Invoke-Command -ComputerName server01 -ScriptBlock { Get-Process | where
name -match word }
```

This may produce errors if the remote system is not configured to allow remote PowerShell connections. If the remote computer has been enabled to allow PowerShell remoting, you should receive a similar set of results of running Get-Process on the local machine.

Similar to the Windows Task Manager, looking at processes using PowerShell helps review what is using resources on a system. When working with remote systems, PowerShell is very fast to return information.

```
(Get-WmiObject -Class Win32_Process -ComputerName server01 |
where Name -match PowerShell.exe).GetOwner() |
Select-Object Domain, User | Format-List
```

■ **Note** Use the Force. Sometimes you need to use the "force" switch to ensure a process stops when requested. According to the help for Stop-Process, using "force" stops the specified processes without prompting for confirmation. By default, Stop-Process prompts for confirmation before stopping any process that is not owned by the current user. To find the owner of a process, use the Get-WmiObject cmdlet to get the Win32_Process class object that represents the process, and then use the GetOwner method of the object.

Using WMI or CIM to Work with Processes

Windows Management Instrumentation (WMI) and its more recent counterpart, Common Information Model (CIM), are tools that help systems administrators interact with local and remote computers in more detail. Where processes are concerned, they can produce more properties about items and provide a better picture of what is going on with a particular system. This is not true in all cases, but it does prove helpful much of the time, so it makes sense to discuss them here. Because CIM is the more recent of the two, it is covered in this section; however, the same classes used by WMI are available when using CIM.

■ **Note**   Remember that WMI cmdlets are required for PowerShell v2 and earlier, and CIM cmdlets are available in newer versions of PowerShell.

Because WMI is the senior statesman, it gets first billing. Using WMI to access information about system processes provides information not shown by the process cmdlets. For example, WMI can use DCOM to tell you which files are open. The following code points out a file open in Notepad.exe:

```
Get-WmiObject -Class Win32_Process -Filter "Name='Notepad.exe'" |
  Select-Object -ExpandProperty CommandLine
```

There are other properties related to processes, including (but not limited to) the following:

- WorkingSet
- ProcessId
- ProcessName
- Installdate

Some of the properties, such as InstallDate, may not have a value if the application is included with the Windows operating system. To see the complete list of properties and methods, you can pipe the Get-Member command.

Using the CIM cmdlets

The properties available with WMI and DCOM are also available when using the Common Information Model. Using the CIM cmdlets, PowerShell uses the WS-Management service to provide information.

As in the preceding example, CIM can return process information about Notepad.

```
Get-CimInstance -ClassName Win32_Process -Filter "Name='Notepad.exe'"
```

The difference between these methods is how they access a system. In PowerShell 3.0 and higher, the CIM cmdlets allow the use of WSMan; in previous versions of PowerShell, however, DCOM and WMI are required. This allows backward compatibility between versions of PowerShell so that computers that are not upgraded are still accessible.

Without specifying which process you wish to review, running Get-CimInstance -ClassName Win32_Process generates the list of currently running processes. Because it can be executed to pull information from remote computers, it can help research what is running on remote servers or workstations if problems arise.

If the computers you need to work with are running Windows prior to Windows 10, they are running PowerShell 4.0 or earlier. If the PowerShell version is 2.0 or older, WMI cmdlets are required. Newer versions of PowerShell can work with the older cmdlets to ensure that you can write scripts that support older versions of PowerShell.

Using PowerShell instead of GUI-based tools to investigate processes can help extract the information provided to other formats. For example, reports can be created and files can be generated with existing process information. This allows you to compare the processes running on a machine several times per day, or you can even compare the processes that are running on several different computers.

Examining the differences between two systems with similar configurations using process usage data can provide insight into how the system is being used. Although it isn't a perfect solution (because two users might use applications differently), it is a good starting point to examine the running processes on a computer.

Summary

In this chapter, processes were the focus of discussion. We covered how PowerShell can interact with processes to verify what computers are running, starting, and stopping. While there are GUI-based tools for these tasks, sometimes it is useful to get a handle on them quickly from the command line.

In the next chapter, we dive into Windows services, which work in a similar way to processes when using PowerShell, but have different issues and actions associated with them.

CHAPTER 7

■ ■ ■

Review and Manage Services with PowerShell

Services in Microsoft Windows accomplish a great many things behind the scenes. In this chapter, we are going to look at how services can be managed with Microsoft PowerShell. The following is from Microsoft's "Introduction to Window Service Applications" page: "Microsoft Windows services, formerly known as NT services, enable you to create long-running executable applications that run in their own Windows sessions. These services can be automatically started when the computer boots, can be paused and restarted, and do not show any user interface. These features make services ideal for use on a server or whenever you need long-running functionality that does not interfere with other users who are working on the same computer. You can also run services in the security context of a specific user account that is different from the logged-on user or the default computer account." (https://msdn.microsoft.com/en-us/library/d56de412.aspx).

Tools like PowerShell that are included in the Windows platform help IT departments reduce costs in managing their environments. Maintaining skills in these areas can help an organization leverage technology without incurring extra costs in keeping an IT environment working efficiently.

Working with services across your environment using the familiar PowerShell interface improves your response time and helps keep your users and systems functioning efficiently.

Access to Services with PowerShell

Like many other resources that we have looked at so far, accessing services can be done locally or remotely from a single PowerShell window. Services need to run under an account, which can be a local user, a domain user, or the local computer account.

© Derek Schauland, Donald Jacobs 2016
D. Schauland and D. Jacobs, *Troubleshooting Windows Server with PowerShell*,
DOI 10.1007/978-1-4842-1851-8_7

■ **Note**   In versions of Windows Server prior to 2008 R2, a user account with a non-expiring password was the most practical choice for service logon. Since then though, Microsoft introduced Managed Service Accounts (MSAs), which configures an Active Directory service account and links it to a single computer. The password is complex and automatically managed by Active Directory, which means that services on this computer do not need to be managed by the administrator. Information about MSAs is at http://blogs.technet.com/ b/askds/archive/2009/09/10/managed-service-accounts-understanding- implementing-best-practices-and-troubleshooting.aspx.

In Windows Server 2012 R2, the MSA concept was further improved to allow service accounts to be managed across multiple computers using Group Managed Service Accounts. More information is at http://blogs.technet.com/b/askpfeplat/ archive/2012/12/17/windows-server-2012-group-managed-service-accounts.aspx.

Managed Service Accounts are important because they save repetitive administrative work when dealing with services because Windows is able to update service passwords automatically. The credentials that the services use are independent of the credentials that you use to access the server and manage services.

Gathering Service Information

Because services on a Windows server can perform so many helpful (and at times frustrating) actions, being able to get information about services during the troubleshooting process can keep the troubleshooting process moving and provide good data about what might be wrong. Let's look at what PowerShell can do with services.

Actions on Services

Similar to the actions available from the services snap-in on a Windows machine, you can use PowerShell to take the following actions on Windows services:

- Start (bring a service online)
- Stop (take a service off line)
- Restart (stop and start a service)
- Change the startup type of a service

Working with services is a required skill set for Windows Server administration. You should be able to manage services without using GUI-based tools and to work on multiple servers at once. PowerShell reduces the overhead for managing services, saves time across an environment, and simplifies the automation of management for environments of all shapes and sizes.

PowerShell is fairly straightforward when it comes to services; there are cmdlets available for manipulating them. As we noted in the previous section, getting information about services also has a cmdlet to use.

Bringing the information to other actions using the pipeline allows discovery and actions in one step.

Let's start by looking at the help for the Get-Service cmdlet shown in Figure 7-1.

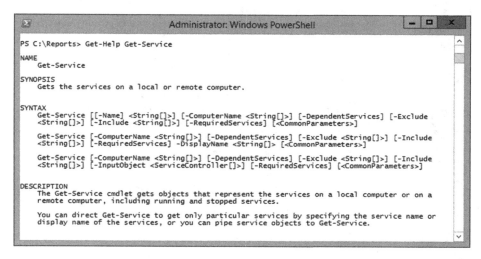

Figure 7-1. *Get-Help Get-Service*

As you can see, you can run against the local computer and remote computers, and get dependent services for each service. For example, to determine if the spooler service is running on a print server and to restart the service to ensure smooth sailing of all printed documents, you could use this:

```
Get-Service | where Name -Match 'spooler' | Restart-Service
```

If the service you have chosen to restart requires dependent services to restart as well, if you use the -Force switch, PowerShell will wait for the dependent items to restart as well and then perform the action on the selected service. If the service is in use and needs elevation the shell will error and alert you that more access is required. In the case of the print spooler, the service restarts without any fanfare and no additional output.

When examining the memberships of the Get-Service cmdlet, you can see there are a few important items as seen in Figure 7-2.

```
┌─────────────────────────────────────────────────────────────────────────┐
│ ⊠                     Administrator: Windows PowerShell      [ _ ][ □ ][ X ]│
├─────────────────────────────────────────────────────────────────────────┤
│ PS C:\Reports> Get-Service | Get-Member                                   │
│                                                                           │
│    TypeName: System.ServiceProcess.ServiceController                      │
│                                                                           │
│ Name                        MemberType    Definition                      │
│ ----                        ----------    ----------                      │
│ Name                        AliasProperty Name = ServiceName              │
│ RequiredServices            AliasProperty RequiredServices = ServicesDependedOn│
│ Disposed                    Event         System.EventHandler Disposed(System.Object, System.Event...│
│ Close                       Method        void Close()                    │
│ Continue                    Method        void Continue()                 │
│ CreateObjRef                Method        System.Runtime.Remoting.ObjRef CreateObjRef(type request...│
│ Dispose                     Method        void Dispose(), void IDisposable.Dispose()│
│ Equals                      Method        bool Equals(System.Object obj)  │
│ ExecuteCommand              Method        void ExecuteCommand(int command)│
│ GetHashCode                 Method        int GetHashCode()               │
│ GetLifetimeService          Method        System.Object GetLifetimeService()│
│ GetType                     Method        type GetType()                  │
│ InitializeLifetimeService   Method        System.Object InitializeLifetimeService()│
│ Pause                       Method        void Pause()                    │
│ Refresh                     Method        void Refresh()                  │
│ Start                       Method        void Start(), void Start(string[] args)│
│ Stop                        Method        void Stop()                     │
│ WaitForStatus               Method        void WaitForStatus(System.ServiceProcess.ServiceControll...│
│ CanPauseAndContinue         Property      bool CanPauseAndContinue {get;} │
│ CanShutdown                 Property      bool CanShutdown {get;}         │
│ CanStop                     Property      bool CanStop {get;}             │
│ Container                   Property      System.ComponentModel.IContainer Container {get;}│
│ DependentServices           Property      System.ServiceProcess.ServiceController[] DependentServi...│
│ DisplayName                 Property      string DisplayName {get;set;}  │
│ MachineName                 Property      string MachineName {get;set;}  │
│ ServiceHandle               Property      System.Runtime.InteropServices.SafeHandle ServiceHandle ...│
│ ServiceName                 Property      string ServiceName {get;set;}  │
│ ServicesDependedOn          Property      System.ServiceProcess.ServiceController[] ServicesDepend...│
│ ServiceType                 Property      System.ServiceProcess.ServiceType ServiceType {get;}│
│ Site                        Property      System.ComponentModel.ISite Site {get;set;}│
│ Status                      Property      System.ServiceProcess.ServiceControllerStatus Status {get;}│
│ ToString                    ScriptMethod  System.Object ToString();      │
│                                                                           │
│ PS C:\Reports> _                                                          │
└─────────────────────────────────────────────────────────────────────────┘
```

Figure 7-2. *Get-Service | Get-Member*

Some of the important properties from Get-Service include CanShutdown, CanStop, DependentServices, and Status. Two of the important methods are Start and Stop.

This means that you can check for dependent services and stop and start services simply by using the Get-Service cmdlet, as shown in Figure 7-3.

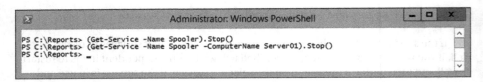

```
┌─────────────────────────────────────────────────────────────────────────┐
│ ⊠                     Administrator: Windows PowerShell      [ _ ][ □ ][ X ]│
├─────────────────────────────────────────────────────────────────────────┤
│ PS C:\Reports> (Get-Service -Name Spooler).Stop()                         │
│ PS C:\Reports> (Get-Service -Name Spooler -ComputerName Server01).Stop()  │
│ PS C:\Reports> _                                                          │
└─────────────────────────────────────────────────────────────────────────┘
```

Figure 7-3. *Stopping services using Get-Service*

When run on a local computer, the service restarted and there was no other output.

Some services do not need to be restarted. Suppose that you want to stop the Microsoft SQL Server service to ensure that there is no access to the databases while you perform maintenance on a server. In this instance, the service should stay stopped until restarted deliberately or until the next system restart. PowerShell can do this easily.

Figure 7-4 shows the Get-Service cmdlet where the service name matches SQL.

```
                      Administrator: Windows PowerShell                    _  □  X

PS C:\Reports> Get-Service | where Name -Match sql

Status    Name               DisplayName
------    ----               -----------
Running   MSSQLFDLauncher    SQL Full-text Filter Daemon Launche...
Running   MSSQLSERVER        SQL Server (MSSQLSERVER)
Stopped   SQLBrowser         SQL Server Browser
Running   SQLCloudAdapter    SQL Server Cloud Adapter
Stopped   SQLSERVERAGENT     SQL Server Agent (MSSQLSERVER)
Running   SQLWriter          SQL Server VSS Writer


PS C:\Reports> _
```

Figure 7-4. *Find SQL services*

■ **Note**   In Figure 7-4, we use the default SQL Server instance on the server.

Once we know the name and the status of the service, we can interact with it:

```
Get-Service -Name MSSQLSERVER | Stop-Service
```

SQL Server has several services that perform work in a SQL environment. For example, the SQL Server Agent service makes backups of databases (among other things). These services depend on SQL Server. If you restart SQL Server and the agent service is running, you may receive a warning that there are dependent services running. If you include the -Force parameter, PowerShell stops any dependent services along with the parent service.

Stopping a service when other services depend on it causes PowerShell to pause. You see an error if you stop a service that has dependency, unless you use the -Force switch.

Once you know that the service has stopped, you can perform the needed maintenance on the server and then use similar commands to get SQL Server up and running again:

```
Get-Service -Name MSSQLSERVER | Start-Service
```

Any dependent services required by SQL Server are also started. It is a good idea to check on them to ensure that they are in the necessary state for your needs.

Start, stop, and restart are the most useful actions when working with services, but there are a few other cmdlets for managing services:

- New-Service
- Set-Service
- Resume-Service
- Suspend-Service

93

New-Service registers a new service in the registry and the service database on a Windows system. When used, there must be an executable file to run while the service is running. If you have an executable that is best run as a service, this is the way to add it to the registry and the service database. When you are done using the service, it can be deleted from the registry so that it does not consume resources. Unfortunately, there is no native PowerShell cmdlet to remove a service, so you need to use an alternative, like this:

```
Sc.exe delete ServiceName
```

Or this:

```
(Get-WmiObject -Class Win32_Service -Filter "Name = 'ServiceName'").Delete()
```

■ **Note**   SC is a command-line program used for communicating with the Service Control Manager and services. It is part of the installed applications, so it is probably already on your computers.

The Set-Service cmdlet allows some properties of a service to be modified.

As you can see in Figure 7-5, you can change the description, display name, start up type, and status.

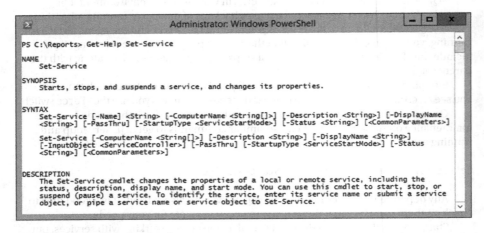

Figure 7-5. *Get-Help Set-Service*

As seen in Figure 7-6, we set the service using the Set-Service cmdlet, but the Get-Service cmdlet was unable to query the description; we had to use WMI to find the description.

```
Administrator: Windows PowerShell                    — □ X

PS C:\Reports> Set-Service -Name Spooler -Description "I Changed the description!"
PS C:\Reports> Get-Service -Name Spooler | Format-List -Property Name, DisplayName, Description


Name        : Spooler
DisplayName : Print Spooler


PS C:\Reports> Get-WmiObject -Class Win32_Service -Filter "Name = 'Spooler'" | Format-List -Property
    Name, DisplayName, Description


Name        : Spooler
DisplayName : Print Spooler
Description : I Changed the description!
```

Figure 7-6. *Example Set-Service*

The Suspend-Service cmdlet pauses a running service, which typically continues to service existing connections but does not accept new connections. Resume-Service removes the pause status of a service to allow new connections from clients. This is different from the Restart-Service cmdlet because Suspend-Service does not stop and start the service.

```
Suspend-Service -Name spooler | Start-Sleep -Seconds 30 | Resume-Service
```

The previous example pauses the spooler service, waits for 30 seconds, and resumes the service.

Enter WMI

Services have a number of cmdlets to return information and manage their state, but WMI and CIM can extend this functionality even further. When a service needs to interact with other systems on a network, for example, things dealing with mail or other widely used items, the account used by the service should be able to interact with the domain, either by being a user account in the domain or by being a Managed Service Account (the preferred option). Since there is not a great way to modify the account or its password with the service cmdlets, many administrators dig into the services management console to change the account, but there is no need. Windows Management Instrumentation (WMI) can help with this for sure.

Let's change the user account information for the famed spooler service.

```
$spoolerService = Get-WmiObject -Class Win32_Service -ComputerName Server01 `
 -Filter "Name = 'spooler'"
```

This sets the spoolerService variable with the spooler service object. Doing this simplifies manipulation because the object is stored in memory and we don't have to continually query the computer for the same information. Now that the variable is created, we can view all the available methods on the object that are associated with the Win32_Service WMI object. This returns all the properties and methods available for the

95

object stored in the spoolerService variable, as noted in Figure 7-7. There are quite a few options available so we won't list them all, but the method we are interested in for the logon account is the Change method.

```
Administrator: Windows PowerShell
PS C:\Reports> $spoolerService = Get-WmiObject –Class Win32_Service –ComputerName Server01 –Filter
Name = 'spooler'"
PS C:\Reports> $spoolerService | Get-Member


   TypeName: System.Management.ManagementObject#root\cimv2\Win32_Service

Name                      MemberType     Definition
----                      ----------     ----------
PSComputerName            AliasProperty  PSComputerName = __SERVER
Change                    Method         System.Management.ManagementBaseObject Change(System.Strin...
ChangeStartMode           Method         System.Management.ManagementBaseObject ChangeStartMode(Sys...
Delete                    Method         System.Management.ManagementBaseObject Delete()
GetSecurityDescriptor     Method         System.Management.ManagementBaseObject GetSecurityDescript...
InterrogateService        Method         System.Management.ManagementBaseObject InterrogateService()
PauseService              Method         System.Management.ManagementBaseObject PauseService()
ResumeService             Method         System.Management.ManagementBaseObject ResumeService()
SetSecurityDescriptor     Method         System.Management.ManagementBaseObject SetSecurityDescript...
StartService              Method         System.Management.ManagementBaseObject StartService()
StopService               Method         System.Management.ManagementBaseObject StopService()
UserControlService        Method         System.Management.ManagementBaseObject UserControlService(...
AcceptPause               Property       bool AcceptPause {get;set;}
AcceptStop                Property       bool AcceptStop {get;set;}
Caption                   Property       string Caption {get;set;}
CheckPoint                Property       uint32 CheckPoint {get;set;}
CreationClassName         Property       string CreationClassName {get;set;}
Description               Property       string Description {get;set;}
DesktopInteract           Property       bool DesktopInteract {get;set;}
DisplayName               Property       string DisplayName {get;set;}
ErrorControl              Property       string ErrorControl {get;set;}
ExitCode                  Property       uint32 ExitCode {get;set;}
InstallDate               Property       string InstallDate {get;set;}
Name                      Property       string Name {get;set;}
PathName                  Property       string PathName {get;set;}
ProcessId                 Property       uint32 ProcessId {get;set;}
ServiceSpecificExitCode   Property       uint32 ServiceSpecificExitCode {get;set;}
ServiceType               Property       string ServiceType {get;set;}
Started                   Property       bool Started {get;set;}
StartMode                 Property       string StartMode {get;set;}
StartName                 Property       string StartName {get;set;}
State                     Property       string State {get;set;}
Status                    Property       string Status {get;set;}
SystemCreationClassName   Property       string SystemCreationClassName {get;set;}
SystemName                Property       string SystemName {get;set;}
```

Figure 7-7. WMI object Win32_Service members

■ **Note**   If you list all of the methods for this WMI object, you see other items that can stop, start, and otherwise act on service objects, much like other cmdlets discussed in this chapter.

Now that we know the method needed to reset the logon information, we can jump right in. These properties are handled in order, which means that we need to pass a null value to the properties that we do not want to change. To find out which parameters are available for modification, run this command:

```
$spoolerService | Get-Member -Name Change | Format-List
```

This highlights the Change method and shows its properties in a list. Doing this makes the entirety of parameters somewhat easier to read, as shown in Figure 7-8.

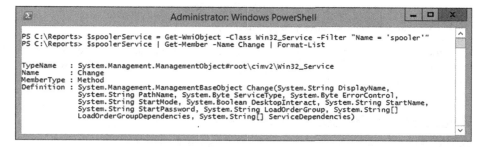

Figure 7-8. *Change method of Win32_Service*

As you can see, there are a number of parameters ahead of the StartName and StartPassword fields. Regarding the Change method of the Win32_Service class, according to MSDN at https://msdn.microsoft.com/en-us/library/windows/desktop/aa384901.aspx, the StartName is defined as the "account name the service runs under" and the StartPassword is the "password to the account name specified by the StartName parameter". Since the Change method is expecting that it may need to act on all of these parameters, we have to pass a $null value for each field that we don't want to change. In Figure 7-9, the command only updates the StartName and StartPassword for the service, leaving all other parameters unchanged.

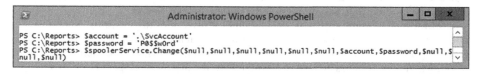

Figure 7-9. *Changing username and password for a service*

As seen in Figure 7-8, the following are the other fields you can change using the Change method:

- System.String DisplayName

- System.String PathName

- System.Byte ServiceType

- System.Byte ErrorControl

- System.String StartMode

- System.Boolean DesktopInteract

- System.String StartName

- System.String StartPassword

- System.String LoadOrderGroup

- System.String[] LoadOrderGroupDependencies

- System.String[] ServiceDependencies

Once the parameters have been changed, the service needs to be restarted to update them. Even when you make changes using the GUI, the same restart is required when modifying the account for a service.

What Else Can Be Done to Services?

Earlier, when we were looking at SQL Server, we noted that it has dependencies. Dependencies are other services that the primary service requires to be running for its own operation. Dependent services are restarted (or stopped) as needed when the service that depends on them is restarted (or stopped). Because they are required by a parent service, this happens automatically for the most part. If for some reason these do not act as expected, they need to be managed independently to ensure the proper operation of the parent service.

Why Services Have Dependencies

Some services rely on other services to perform functions used in their operation. The SQL Server Agent service performs backup tasks and other management services within SQL software. Think of this situation much the same way as functions that exist inside a PowerShell module. SQL Server Agent is dependent on SQL Server.

PowerShell functions are typically at their best when they do one thing. Not only does this produce code that is less prone to errors, but it also helps with readability. Grouping related functions into a module allows them to be loaded into memory, working together. Services behave in a similar way: the SQL Server Agent handles a subset of functions within SQL Server, allowing the busier SQL Server service to focus on database engine tasks. This helps isolate tasks in memory and it improves performance and functionality.

Reporting on Services or Providing More Presentable Information

Like other things PowerShell provides, reporting is more about formatting and output files than it is about PowerShell specifically. Because PowerShell can send data to a number of file formats and output files, it is very versatile in reporting the information collected. On top of that, the ability to send the results via email to a manager or colleagues is extremely helpful.

Since we worked with an HTML file in Chapter 6, this time, we will push the output to a comma-separated values (CSV) file. Although there is less flash with this file type, its ease of import and use in other applications makes it quite useful.

Scenario: Your manager has asked for a list of services running on a handful of servers because performance problems across applications are being reported. Your manager wants to ensure that no extraneous services running on the servers and that the required services *are* running. Because this data collection is ongoing and the data will be compared over a number of weeks, your manager asks that the data is presented in a way that can be imported into a database for easy comparison and number crunching.

Because PowerShell can act against multiple remote servers, the Get-Service cmdlet allows you to query more than one computer using a single line of code.

```
Get-Service -ComputerName server01, server02, server03
```

This line of code provides a list of the services on each of the servers. When the data is returned, the service grouping from server01 is shown first, with server02 and server03 following respectively. Since you were asked only for running services, there is some additional work to do. Let's use Invoke-Command.

```
Get-service –computername server01. Server02, server03 | where status –eq running
```

The data is returned in the order the remote systems are specified; but this time, only running services are returned.

That's great. You have the running services for the three servers listed. Now you can get them out to a file.

```
Get-Service -ComputerName server01. Server02, server03 |
  where Status -EQ Running |
  Export-Csv -Path "c:\reports\services-list.csv" -NoTypeInformation
```

However, this data does not pipe into a flat CSV file easily. You need to do advanced formatting on some of the fields to put the output to a CSV file. By examining which fields have multiple values returned using the Get-Member cmdlet, you see that three fields are returning more than one value for a single property. You can select all the properties and use advanced formatting to make the data look better in the CSV file by running this command:

```
Get-Service -ComputerName server01. Server02, server03 |
 where Status -EQ Running |
 Select-Object -Property Name,
  @{Name = 'RequiredServices' ; Expression = { $_.RequiredServices -join ';'}},
  CanPauseAndContinue,
  CanShutdown,
  CanStop,
  DisplayName,
  @{Name='DependentServices';Expression = { $_.DependentServices -join ';'}},
  MachineName,
  ServiceName,
  @{Name='ServicesDependedOn';Expression = { $_.ServicesDependedOn -join ';'}},
  ServiceHandle,
  Status,
```

```
ServiceType,
Site,
Container |
Export-Csv -Path "c:\reports\services-list.csv" -NoTypeInformation
```

Simply piping the collected data to an Export-Csv and providing a path to park the file will get the data out. The addition of the -NoTypeInformation switch omits the type information from the CSV file.

So we have pulled information about running services from three servers and created a CSV file of it. The last thing to do is build a way to email the file to those who have requested it.

■ **Note**   PowerShell could push this information into a SQL database directly, but that is beyond the scope of this book. For more information on working with SQL Server, please visit https://msdn.microsoft.com/en-us/library/hh245198.aspx

---

The Send-MailMessage cmdlet will be used to email the results of this data collection to those who need it. Grouping everything in this scenario into a script looks something like this:

```
$services = Get-Service -ComputerName server01, server02, server03 |
 where Status -EQ Running
$services |
 Select-Object -Property Name,
  @{Name = 'RequiredServices' ; Expression = { $_.RequiredServices -join ';'}},
  CanPauseAndContinue,
  CanShutdown,
  CanStop,
  DisplayName,
  @{Name = 'DependentServices';Expression = { $_.DependentServices -join ';'}},
  MachineName,
  ServiceName,
  @{Name = 'ServicesDependedOn';Expression = { $_.ServicesDependedOn -join ';'}},
  ServiceHandle,
  Status,
  ServiceType,
  Site,
  Container |
 Export-Csv -Path "c:\reports\services-list.csv" -NoTypeInformation
Send-MailMessage -To boss@your.company.suffix `
 -Cc you@your.company.suffix `
 -SmtpServer smtp.company.com `
 -From reports@your.company.suffix `
 -Subject 'Services Listing from Servers' `
 -Body 'List of services running on Server01, Server02, and Server03' `
 -Attachments "c:\reports\services-list.csv"
```

Summary

This chapter worked with Windows services by using PowerShell to determine the information available and the actions needed to improve the manageability of Microsoft Windows. While the behavior of services is similar to that of processes, PowerShell can speed up the time needed to perform actions and reduce management overhead. Coming up in the next chapter, we wrap up the book and provide some additional resources to help you learn more and enhance your use of PowerShell.

CHAPTER 8

■ ■ ■

Continuing to Learn As PowerShell Evolves

So far in this book, we have shown you how to

- Work with event logs

- Gather detailed information from a server

- Discover installed applications

- Get Windows updates

- Manage running processes

- Work with services

There's a lot of good information here to glean information from a computer both locally and remotely. In this chapter, we'll talk about putting them together and ways to build this knowledge into more robust scripting.

Building Modules

PowerShell coding starts simple, usually with only a few lines of PowerShell. That evolves into a script when you start adding more features to ultimately achieve the goal for the script. As you write more scripts, and continue learning and using PowerShell, you will inevitably want to reuse parts of your scripts in other scripts, and therefore you create functions. A *function* is just a block of code that does one thing, such as running a formula, gathering information, or performing a repetitive task.

As you gain more and more functions that all work together with a common purpose, you put those into a *module*. Microsoft describes a module as "a set of related Windows PowerShell functionalities that can be dynamic or persist on disk. Modules that persist on disk are referenced, loaded, and persisted as script modules, binary modules, or manifest modules. Unlike snap-ins, the members of these modules can include cmdlets, providers, functions, variables, aliases, and much more." (https://technet.microsoft.com/en-us/library/dd878324.aspx).

A quick example of a module is preparing food. How is food an example? Easy, let's say that you're hungry. The following are some example names of functions that you could use in your food module:

- Set-Stove, where you can pass it variables such as temperature, burners, oven, and so forth

- Set-Ingredient, where you pass it variables that include the ingredients that you need for a specific recipe

- Get-Dish, where you pass variables about the items that you need to make the food in

- ConvertTo-Baking, where you determine how to bake food

- Get-CookingDirection, where you describe how to cook the food

All of these functions have a common theme: cooking. Likewise, you could have a module for driving a car, and those functions would all be associated with ... (drumroll please) driving a car. There may be some overlap in the background functions, such as report writing and diagnostics, but for the most part, each module has a specific purpose and the parts that make up the module are all devoted to making the best module they can.

So, we are going to build a quick simple module called HelloWorld. It's going to be a very simple module that consists of only two functions.

```
Function Write-Hello {
  param ($Name)
  Write-Output "Hello '$Name'"
}

Function Write-Goodbye {
  param ($Name)
  Write-Output "Goodbye '$Name'"
}
```

Notice how simple this is? It's nothing to get excited about—just an example of two functions. Now we are going to save this inside a PSM1 file (PowerShell Module file). But the next question is: Where to save the PSM1 file?

We need to find a location for PowerShell modules, which are listed as an environmental variable for our PowerShell session. Simply type **$env:PSModulePath** and it lists all the locations where you can have PowerShell modules. However, we can do a little better than that and split that long string into shorter lines by typing this:

```
$env:PSModulePath -split ';'
```

We can also add a location to our PowerShell module path by typing this:

```
$env:PSModulePath = $env:PSModulePath + ";\\Server\Share\Modules"
```

So, why don't we create a new folder and save our module there.

```
New-Item -Path c:\MyModules -ItemType Directory
$env:PSModulePath = $env:PSModulePath + ";c:\MyModules"
```

Because we created a new folder that is not already in our PSModulePath, the known path that PowerShell uses for storing modules, we recommend adding this to your PowerShell profile so that the path is always added to your PowerShell session. Another method is to add these items to a system-level environment variable to allow persistence across sessions.

Now we can save our two functions inside a PSM1 file inside the new folder. However, we need to save our PSM1 file inside a folder with the same name as our PSM1, at the root of the C:\MyModules folder. For our example, you need to create a folder at C:\MyModules\HelloWorld and then save the PSM1 file as C:\MyModules\HelloWorld\HelloWorld.psm1.

Now that we have updated our PowerShell profile file to add that folder to our PSModulePath environmental variable and saved our PSM1 file, let's close and open the PowerShell session. Now, if you are running PowerShell version 3 or later, the module will automatically load when you start your PowerShell session.

As seen in Figure 8-1, we can simply run those without having to load the module each time.

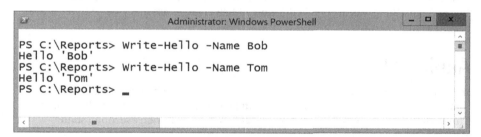

Figure 8-1. *Example of running commands in new module*

There are a lot of other parts and pieces to a module that we haven't discussed, but this is the start to a world of building modules. We can simply add features to the module.

Desired State Configuration

Have you ever had a server that was configured just the way you always wanted it, only to deploy it into production and have its nice configuration marred by actual usage? Maybe that is a bit extreme, but sometimes machines wander away from their original setup. Or maybe another administrator decides to alter the current configuration. Desired State Configuration to the rescue!

■ **Note** This discussion of PowerShell Desired State Configuration is an overview containing just enough to rile your interest in the topic.

What Is Desired State Configuration (DSC)?

Desired State Configuration is a declarative file that instructs PowerShell to ensure that a system is configured with the roles and features or configuration options set forth in the file. The file does not tell PowerShell how to get there; it simply says, "This is the configuration that I want. Go." And PowerShell does the rest.

A configuration file is compiled into a MOF (Management Object Format) when it is run. The MOF can then be deployed to target nodes for use in one of two ways: push or pull.

Push happens when a DSC configuration uses the push method; targets are configured to take the settings pushed down to them at scheduled intervals. Think of this much like patches being pushed out by a corporate administrator because they will correct a problem as soon as they are deployed. Sure, the push can be scheduled, but it can also have interesting consequences regarding the usability of the systems. It should be used and tested carefully.

Pull happens when a DSC configuration uses the pull method; targets get an agent installed that periodically checks in with a central location (pull server) for configurations to apply. Because the files are usually left there, the clients can pull the files and be configured according to all of the MOF files that they are aware of.

Configurations are applied each time the targets check in (or each time the MOFs are pushed out). There is no need to instruct file 12 to be applied. If the configuration provided by file 12 does not need to be corrected, the action logs back to the central server that nothing was needed at this time. When changes are made by DSC, these are logged as well.

Auditing Only

In addition to push/pull, DSC has two modes of action for working on target systems. *Audit mode* checks a configuration against the target and reports changes that it made. This is similar (in a simple way) to the -whatif switch used when executing some PowerShell commands.

Applying Configurations: Make It So

When not using Audit mode, DSC applies items in the MOF files to all the targets assigned to take them. If you have an IIS server enrolled with a pull server, any MOFs containing IIS configuration items are applied to this target. There are ways to ensure that only certain configurations apply to certain targets, but that is beyond the scope of this chapter.

What Does a DSC Configuration Look Like?

The syntax for creating a DSC configuration looks much like the syntax for a function in PowerShell:

```
configuration troubleshootingiis {
  param($ComputerName)
  node $ComputerName {
    windowsfeature iis {
      ensure = "Present"
      name = "web-server"
    }
  }
}
```

Essentially, you are able to pass the $computer value to the configuration. This will then enact the settings within the configuration on that node. In this case, it ensures that IIS is present on this node.

Calling the configuration (just as you might call a function) creates the consumable MOF file for use with DSC:

```
Troubleshootingiis -ComputerName MyServer01
```

The last piece of the puzzle is running the configuration and applying the MOF file. To do that, you call the Start-DscConfiguration and pass the MOF file created. Specifying the -wait and -verbose switches show you what is happening during the process.

What Are Some Practical Applications of DSC?

Because DSC is declarative and does not supply any details of how something is to be accomplished, the configurations simply state that a feature needs to be configured. In the preceding example, DSC simply knows IIS should be present. Why is this important? Because it allows PowerShell to figure out the method to complete a task, saving administrators from extra work.

Starting or Stopping Services

If there is a server in your environment that runs a particular service that does not always start as expected, DSC ensures that the service is started (or stopped) every time the agent checks in. This keeps the service in a consistent state—either started or stopped as declared by DSC.

Installing Necessary Roles or Features

When spinning up a new server to be used for a particular workload, the desired roles/features can be configured by DSC without additional configuration by the administrator. This way, the configuration for all of your web servers is the same. Once the machine is built and able to check in with the DSC server, the web server configuration can be configured automatically. This takes some additional front-end work to set up the DSC MOF files, but it can save time if there are many servers being deployed with the same workload.

Fixing Configuration Drift: Wrongly Installed Applications

Many times, a server ends up with its configuration different from the way it started life—as a valued worker in an environment. This could be due to application changes, updates, or countless other things. DSC can correct these things as well. Suppose one of the administrators on a given team always installs Chrome on every machine that he manages. Yet, it might not be a supported application or it may be unnecessary on a server system. PowerShell and DSC can ensure that Chrome is not present on a particular server. As long as the machine can get to the DSC server and it gets a MOF that specifies that Chrome not be present, the application will be removed from the server.

Ensuring That Files or Folders Exist

Sometimes it makes sense for a particular tool to be installed on a system. This may be simply to ensure that the tools are there if needed or to get an administrator's system up and running with the latest tools. The Sysinternals tools are a great example. Because the tools do not need to install to function, they can be downloaded to a central file server. DSC can ensure that the downloaded files exist on all administrative workstations. Just apply a MOF that ensures the presence of the Sysinternals folder. Since any items removed from the folder are replaced when the workstation checks in, the worry of ensuring that the tools exist is eliminated.

All of these relate to troubleshooting, but how are they applied? DSC can help with all of the things mentioned earlier. Now let's pick an example relating to IIS being installed on a server destined to host the next great web application.

Working with DSC to Ensure IIS Is Installed

Suppose that your environment has a few IIS web sites running on a server and you need to add a bit more horsepower. You allow the workload to be divided up between the existing server and a new server that will be deployed. A co-worker has been tasked with getting IIS installed and he claims that the box is ready to tackle any workload.

Just to be on the good side of the fence, you want to ensure that IIS is indeed installed and running. Fortunately, DSC cannot only help perform the check, but it can correct the issue and configure IIS if it needs a bit of work.

First is testing the existing configuration on the new server to see if IIS is ready. For the purposes of example, let's call it Server02.

Earlier we created a MOF called troubleshootingiis, which creates a file that will become a configuration to check for here. The following command

```
Test-dscconfiguration –cimsession Server02
```

checks Server02 to see if it meets the desired configuration; in this case, a configured IIS instance. If the feature is in fact ready to go, the command returns $true. If not, the command returns $false.

If the previous command returns $false and IIS has not been installed, or you want to check the state and correct it all at once, you can get PowerShell and DSC to rectify this by using something similar to the following:

```
If ( -not (Test-DscConfiguration -CimSession Server02)) {
  Start-DscConfiguration -CimSession Server02
}
```

This applies the current configuration, troubleshootingiis, to the specified server.

■ **Note**   Leaving -cimsession off of either of these commands will run the dscconfiguration cmdlets on the local computer.

What happens if you decide that the new configuration is not what you really intended? Fortunately, PowerShell has a way to recover from over-eager configurations. Simply using Restore-DscConfiguration -CimSession Server02 rolls the configuration back to the previous state.

Desired State Configuration can do a lot of things beyond enabling IIS, and the overall usage is not a huge undertaking, but getting much beyond that is a topic for another day.

PowerShell Remoting

Using PowerShell to troubleshoot and remediate issues on Windows computers would be less than optimal if there were no good way to access systems outside of the local computer. Enter PowerShell Remoting—a built-in feature to help PowerShell interact with remote systems and execute commands, scripts, and the like to reduce the effort needed to manage and maintain remote systems.

This section introduces the concept of remoting and provides a high-level overview of what the feature brings to the toolkit. Because it is built into PowerShell version 2 and later, it generally works once it has been enabled.

How Do I Enable Remoting?

Enabling remoting was already briefly mentioned in the book, but for completeness, we'll cover it here as well. The first thing needed is the WinRM service. You want to set the startup type of this service to Automatic. On the remote system, you can run `winrm quickconfig` to ensure that the WinRM service is listening.

Then you need to run the simple and quite instructive `Enable-PSRemoting` to complete the configuration of Windows PowerShell for remoting. In a domain environment, you can also enable PowerShell remoting using Group Policy.

In untrusted domains, there may be other configuration steps needed to get remoting up and running. You will want to add the remote computer to the trusted hosts list on your management workstation. To do this use the following command:

```
Set-Item WSMan:\localhost\Client\TrustedHosts -value Server01
```

This adds Server01 to the trusted hosts list on the local computer. Once this is done, remoting is all set and ready to go. Happy remoting.

Now that PowerShell remoting is enabled, what can you do with it?

Remoting brings you all kinds of possibilities for managing systems. While the `-ComputerName` parameter lets you do things like gather services (or other items) and display them in your console for reviewing, using a remote PowerShell session lands you right on that system at the command line, as if you were logged into the computer.

Let's get into a remote session by using the command `Enter-PSSession`, as shown in Figure 8-2.

Figure 8-2. Enter-PSSession

A Remote PowerShell Session

As you can see, the PowerShell prompt shows the folder that you are currently in, but this time, it also has the computer name at the left of the prompt: [Server01]. This tells you that you are on a remote computer. Commands entered while in this session are run on that remote system and do not affect the local system.

This is a benefit because you can work directly on the remote computer to solve problems. In addition, you can leave a session running in the background and long-running PowerShell scripts or commands will continue to run inside the disconnected session. You can revisit the disconnected session to see how things there are progressing.

The ability to get in and out of remote sessions while tasks are progressing is very important because it allows other work to get done without requiring you to wait for the task in the console window to complete. Once remoting for a while, you can advance to entering and running commands in multiple sessions sequentially, or in some cases, simultaneously.

Remoting is a simple way to work with any Windows machine in your environment. Environments outside of your direct control are also on the table. Machines in public cloud environments, such as Microsoft Azure or Amazon Web Services (AWS), can be managed with PowerShell remoting.

While there are other PowerShell remoting features, these are the basics, and should head you down the right path.

Using Scheduled Jobs in PowerShell

PowerShell background jobs were introduced in PowerShell version 2. PowerShell scheduled jobs rely on the background jobs, but in PowerShell version 3, the ability to schedule a background job was added. PowerShell scheduled jobs are a combination of background jobs and tasks in the Task Scheduler. The jobs are created and managed in PowerShell and are seen within the Task Scheduler.

Scheduled jobs ensure that certain things start or happen at a specific time. PowerShell is helpful with troubleshooting, but there may be times when restarting services or entire servers cannot occur. A scheduled job could be just the thing to restart a service or end a process as a delayed part of your troubleshooting process/workflow.

Scheduled jobs consist of three components:

- Job options that define the options and execution criteria.

- Job triggers that define when the job will run.

- The job itself defines the command that will run.

You have to define the job options, create a job trigger, and then when creating the job, add the options and trigger to it.

Scheduled Jobs Options

The, New-ScheduledJobOption cmdlet is used to create the job options. As seen in Figure 8-3, there are several switches and parameters that you can use to customize your scheduled job.

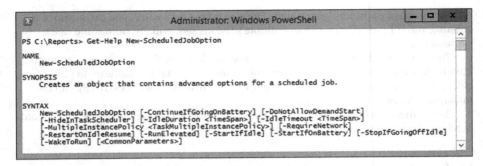

Figure 8-3. Syntax for New-ScheduledJobOption

You create an option and add it to a variable.

```
$jobOption = New-ScheduledJobOption -RequireNetwork -WakeToRun -RunElevated
```

Scheduled Job Triggers

The job trigger defines when the job will run. As seen in Figure 8-4, there are five parameter sets used for the job triggers.

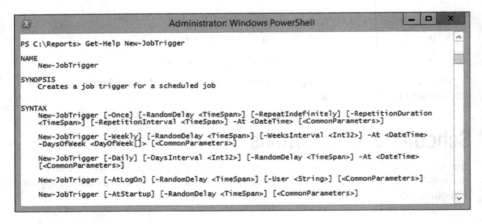

Figure 8-4. Syntax for New-JobTrigger

Adding the job triggers to a variable is the next step in creating a scheduled job.

```
$jobTrigger = New-JobTrigger -Weekly -DaysOfWeek Monday, Tuesday, Wednesday,
Thursday, Friday -At '1:00AM'
```

Creating the Scheduled Job

The Register-ScheduledJob cmdlet takes the job options and the job trigger, and adds them with a script block to create a scheduled job.

```
Register-ScheduledJob -Trigger $jobTrigger `
    -ScheduledJobOption $jobOption `
    -ScriptBlock { Get-Service } `
    -MaxResultCount 5 `
    -Name "ListServices"
```

This code creates a job called ListServices that runs Monday through Friday that keeps only the last five results.

Now there is a scheduled job. The next step verifies that the job exists and gets the results.

Job Verification

To verify that the job exists, you can get a list of scheduled jobs through PowerShell or through the Task Scheduler. Figure 8-5 shows all the jobs that are scheduled and Figure 8-6 shows the same results.

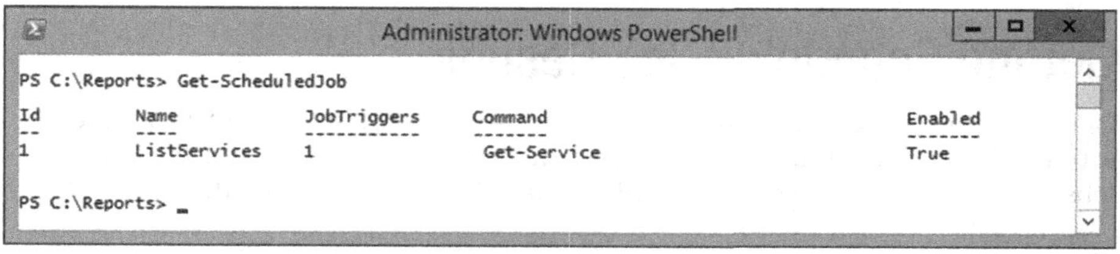

Figure 8-5. *List jobs with PowerShell*

In Figure 8-6, the picture was altered to fit the size of the pages and to find the jobs. You have to drill into the scheduled tasks in this path, Microsoft\Windows\PowerShell\ScheduledJobs to find all the scheduled jobs that were created with PowerShell.

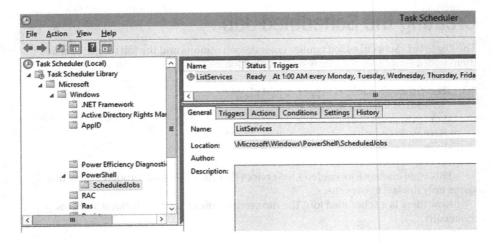

***Figure 8-6.** List jobs in Task Scheduler*

Now that we know the job exists, we can start the schedule job using either the Task Scheduler or PowerShell, and of course, the job will run according to the schedule.

```
Start-Job -DefinitionName ListServices
```

Getting Scheduled Job Results

Once a PowerShell scheduled job has been created and run, the results of the job are saved in the regular PowerShell jobs. As seen in Figure 8-7, it will only save the last five jobs. Even if the job runs again, there will still be only five jobs listed for the job.

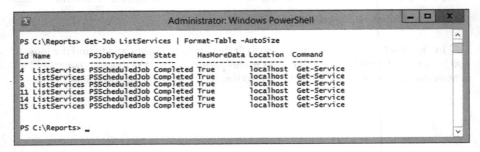

***Figure 8-7.** Job results for a scheduled job*

Also, notice in Figure 8-7 that the HasMoreData values of True. We can retrieve the results of each job by using the `Receive-Job` cmdlet to get the data from each job. This next line will retrieve the results from the most recent version of the job:

```
Receive-Job -Id 15 -Keep
```

Scheduled jobs are a great tool to do routine and repeatable tasks.

More Learning and Additional Resources

We encourage you to dig into the following resources to enhance and continue to grow your PowerShell skills:

- `http://www.powershell.org`: A community of PowerShell, for PowerShell, and by Powershell-ers

- `http://www.scriptingguys.com`: the official blog of the Microsoft Scripting Guys

- `http://www.powershellmagazine.com`: an online publication covering all things PowerShell

- `http://www.apress.com/catalogsearch/result/?q=powershell &submit=Go`: Apress books covering PowerShell

- `https://channel9.msdn.com/Search?term=powershell#ch9Sear ch&lang-en=en`: PowerShell videos on Microsoft's Channel 9

- `https://technet.microsoft.com/en-us/library/ dd878350(v=vs.85).aspx`: Technet resources covering PowerShell Module Installation

There are also any number of user groups and meetups popping up surrounding PowerShell. These should provide a hands-on experience and opportunity to dive into Microsoft's new blue window.

There are many new and exciting avenues for exploration as your adventures in PowerShell continue, we hope that this text has piqued your interest and that you find many exciting things to learn in PowerShell.

Summary

Microsoft is moving forward with PowerShell and expects it to reduce the overhead needed to manage and interact with Windows and other products across their portfolio, including Microsoft Azure. Being able to manage workstations and servers in your environment and in the public cloud with the same toolset is huge. This reduces the overall learning curve for managing resources in use today and new Microsoft resources as they arrive in the future.

As PowerShell continues to grow, more resources will be available for management from Microsoft and other vendors. Happy PowerShelling!

Index

Get the eBook for only $5!

Why limit yourself?

Now you can take the weightless companion with you wherever you go and access your content on your PC, phone, tablet, or reader.

Since you've purchased this print book, we're happy to offer you the eBook in all 3 formats for just $5.

Convenient and fully searchable, the PDF version enables you to easily find and copy code—or perform examples by quickly toggling between instructions and applications. The MOBI format is ideal for your Kindle, while the ePUB can be utilized on a variety of mobile devices.

To learn more, go to www.apress.com/companion or contact support@apress.com.

Printed in the United States
By Bookmasters